CARBON OFFSETTING IN INTERNATIONAL AVIATION IN ASIA AND THE PACIFIC
CHALLENGES AND OPPORTUNITIES

DECEMBER 2020

ASIAN DEVELOPMENT BANK

 Creative Commons Attribution 3.0 IGO license (CC BY 3.0 IGO)

© 2020 Asian Development Bank
6 ADB Avenue, Mandaluyong City, 1550 Metro Manila, Philippines
Tel +63 2 8632 4444; Fax +63 2 8636 2444
www.adb.org

Some rights reserved. Published in 2020.

ISBN 978-92-9262-544-3 (print); 978-92-9262-545-0 (electronic); 978-92-9262-546-7 (ebook)
Publication Stock No. TCS200369-2
DOI: http://dx.doi.org/10.22617/TCS200369-2

The views expressed in this publication are those of the authors and do not necessarily reflect the views and policies of the Asian Development Bank (ADB) or its Board of Governors or the governments they represent.

ADB does not guarantee the accuracy of the data included in this publication and accepts no responsibility for any consequence of their use. The mention of specific companies or products of manufacturers does not imply that they are endorsed or recommended by ADB in preference to others of a similar nature that are not mentioned.

By making any designation of or reference to a particular territory or geographic area, or by using the term "country" in this document, ADB does not intend to make any judgments as to the legal or other status of any territory or area.

This work is available under the Creative Commons Attribution 3.0 IGO license (CC BY 3.0 IGO) https://creativecommons.org/licenses/by/3.0/igo/. By using the content of this publication, you agree to be bound by the terms of this license. For attribution, translations, adaptations, and permissions, please read the provisions and terms of use at https://www.adb.org/terms-use#openaccess.

This CC license does not apply to non-ADB copyright materials in this publication. If the material is attributed to another source, please contact the copyright owner or publisher of that source for permission to reproduce it. ADB cannot be held liable for any claims that arise as a result of your use of the material.

Please contact pubsmarketing@adb.org if you have questions or comments with respect to content, or if you wish to obtain copyright permission for your intended use that does not fall within these terms, or for permission to use the ADB logo.

Corrigenda to ADB publications may be found at http://www.adb.org/publications/corrigenda.

Notes:
In this publication, "$" refers to United States dollars.
ADB recognizes "China" as the People's Republic of China and "Korea" as the Republic of Korea.
This report uses the regional designation "Asia" and "Asia and the Pacific" interchangeably, both terms describe the greater Asia and Pacific region, except for when stated otherwise in the report.

Cover design by Edith Creus.

On the cover, clockwise from left: Burgos Wind and Solar Farm in Ilocos Norte, Philippines (photo by Al Benavente/ADB); Aircraft photo by Freepik; Aerial view of Fiji from a passenger plane (photo by Eric Sales/ADB).

Contents

Tables, Figures, and Boxes ... iv
Foreword ... v
Preface ... vii
Acknowledgments ... ix
Abbreviations ... x
Executive Summary ... xi

1 **Introduction** ... 1
   1.1 Global Emissions from International Aviation ... 1
   1.2 Climate Policy for International Aviation ... 2

2 **Carbon Offsetting and Reduction Scheme for International Aviation** ... 4
   2.1 Rationale for the Offsetting Scheme ... 4
   2.2 Design of the Scheme ... 5
   2.3 Scheme Administration and Transparency ... 6
   2.4 Criteria for Determining the Eligibility of Emission Units ... 7

3 **Offset Supply Outlook for International Aviation** ... 9
   3.1 Paris Agreement and Offset Supply Outlook in All Phases, 2021–2035 ... 9
   3.2 Offset Supply Outlook in the Pilot Phase, 2021–2023 ... 11

4 **Demand Outlook for Offsets by International Aviation and Impact of COVID-19** ... 16
   4.1 The Impact of COVID-19 on International Aviation Traffic ... 16
   4.2 Offset Demand Outlook in All Phases, 2021–2035 ... 18
   4.3 Offset Demand Outlook in the Pilot Phase, 2021–2023 ... 21
   4.4 Offset Demand in Asia and the Pacific ... 23
   4.5 Other Potential Sources of Offset Demand from Aviation ... 27

5 **Challenges and Opportunities for Supplying Offsets from Asia** ... 28
   5.1 Climate Policy Makers in Developing Member Countries ... 28
   5.2 Carbon Offset Suppliers from Developing Member Countries ... 29

Appendixes
   1 Carbon Offsetting and Reduction Scheme for International Aviation Emissions Unit Eligibility Criteria ... 31
   2 Double-Counting Provisions ... 34

References ... 38

Tables, Figures, and Boxes

Tables

1	Clean Development Mechanism Supply of Offsets Compliant to the Carbon Offsetting and Reduction Scheme for International Aviation in the Pilot Phase	14
2	Offset Demand for Select Developing Member Countries, 2021–2026	25
A1	Carbon Offsetting and Reduction Scheme for International Aviation Host Country Attestation and Double-Counting Provisions	34

Figures

1	International Carbon Dioxide Emissions from Commercial Air Transport	2
2	Abatement Cost Curve for Commercial Air Transport in 2030	4
3	Three Design Elements of the Carbon Offsetting and Reduction Scheme for International Aviation	6
4	Overarching Eligibility Criteria for Offsets in the Pilot Phase	12
5	Offset Supply and Demand in the Pilot Phase	13
6	Eligible Clean Development Mechanism Supply During the Pilot Phase	15
7	Impact of COVID-19 Shock on International Aviation Carbon Dioxide Emissions	18
8	Impact of COVID-19 Shock on Offset Demand in All Phases, 2021–2035	19
9	Impact of COVID-19 Shock on Offset Demand in the Pilot Phase	22
10	International Air Traffic Performed by Airlines from Developing Member Countries	23
11	Carbon Offset Demand of Airlines by Region of Registration	24
12	Breakdown of Commercial Air Transport Carbon Dioxide Emissions by Activity	27

Boxes

1	Avoiding Double Counting in the Pilot Phase	10
2	Long-Term Potential of Sustainable Aviation Fuels	21
3	Offsetting Airline Carbon Dioxide Emissions in the Republic of Korea	26

Foreword

The world has been hit by a pandemic that has created a downturn in economic activity, forcing people to change their social life significantly and causing the loss of regular income for many. At the same time, the lockdown response has resulted in a much-needed relief for the earth and its ecosystems, which has opened up an opportunity for a green recovery response.

It is encouraging that this year likely will see a drop in greenhouse gas (GHG) emissions for the first time in many years. However, the concentration of carbon dioxide in the atmosphere continues to increase, implying that mitigation measures must be intensified in all sectors at all levels—international, national, and local—if the goals of the Paris Agreement are to be met.

The aviation sector is an important sector. While only accounting for approximately 2% of global anthropogenic carbon dioxide emissions of which almost two-thirds stem from international flights, the sector has become representative for lifestyle patterns that are regarded as unsustainable. The aviation sector has been heavily affected by the pandemic and for some aspects of life, not least work meetings, it has been proven that flying may not always be necessary. Whether the sector will reach its previous levels of activity, and by when, is debated. In any case, even though the pandemic will put this sector in an extraordinary situation for a few years, international aviation is still likely to grow over time and with that, its emissions.

In October 2016, the International Civil Aviation Organization (ICAO) decided to launch an initiative to limit the emissions from international aviation. Emissions from international transport have been kept out of international climate agreements under the United Nations Framework Convention on Climate Change save for some reporting obligations. As part of a set of measures; including aircraft technology improvements, sustainable aviation fuels, and operational improvements; the Carbon Offsetting and Reduction Scheme for International Aviation (CORSIA) aims to ensure carbon-neutral growth of the aviation sector. This new scheme reflects two important trends in GHG mitigation action.

The first trend is carbon pricing, which now covers 46 national and 32 subnational jurisdictions. Carbon pricing includes cap-and-trade and taxes that imply a cost for the emitter. It also includes offsetting approaches where the supplier of carbon credits will benefit economically from achieving emission reductions. CORSIA will result in a cost for airline operators and through its demand, an opportunity for project owners to sell carbon credits. The important element here is that there is a signal that increased emissions will come with a cost.

The second trend is net zero or carbon neutrality approaches. The world will need to reach net zero GHG emissions early in the second half of this century to meet the Paris Agreement's temperature goals. In the context of the Paris Agreement, achieving net zero emissions means balancing emissions caused by humans and removals of GHGs in a given time period. In the context of international aviation, it means using offsets to mitigate emissions that are difficult to abate, which is an approach typically taken by companies that can reduce some of their emissions, but not all, at least not in the short term.

While several countries already have adopted, and many more are planning to adopt, net zero (or carbon neutrality) targets, the international aviation sector is aiming for net zero growth of emissions. ICAO recognizes that curbing the contribution of aviation to climate change can be achieved more cost-effectively by tapping into the abatement potential in other sectors. It does so by allowing the use of carbon credits from carbon crediting programs that have been approved by ICAO.

This report, *Carbon Offsetting in International Aviation in Asia and the Pacific: Challenges and Opportunities*, highlights the key issues that participants in CORSIA will face, with specific attention paid to the concrete opportunity that will open for developing member countries of the Asian Development Bank to benefit from the sale of carbon offsets, and with specific consideration given the impact of the coronavirus disease. We hope that this report will help Asia and the Pacific to formulate strategies that contribute to enhancing international cooperation to combat climate change.

Woochong Um
Director General
Sustainable Development and Climate Change Department
Asian Development Bank

Preface

In March 2020, the International Civil Aviation Organization (ICAO) approved the list of programs that are eligible to supply carbon credits for offsetting greenhouse gas emissions attributable to international aviation, thus moving a step closer to operationalize the Carbon Offsetting and Reduction Scheme for International Aviation (CORSIA). CORSIA, likely to start from January 2021, will encourage carbon dioxide abatement activities within the international aviation sector while relying on sourcing cost-effective carbon offsets from other sectors. CORSIA currently offers the clearest opportunity in the post-2020 international climate change policy framework through which developing member countries (DMCs) of the Asian Development Bank (ADB) can benefit from participating in international carbon markets.

Thus, there has been hope among project owners that CORSIA would provide a significant demand. However, the coronavirus disease (COVID-19) has resulted in grounding a large share of the global aircraft fleet, which has made the near-term demand highly uncertain. Despite the collapse in air transport activity and expectation for a slow recovery, international aviation is expected to continue to have significant demand for carbon offsets up to at least 2035. Even under scenarios of a slow post-COVID-19 recovery and subdued growth, the sector is expected to demand significant volumes of offsets if it is to meet existing climate targets. Furthermore, if the net carbon dioxide emission trajectory of the sector is to align with the temperature goals of the Paris Agreement, there will be a major increase in offset demand.

For the CORSIA pilot phase (2021–2023), ICAO has approved the use of certain carbon offsets generated from six carbon offset programs, including the Clean Development Mechanism. Projects that start their crediting period after January 2016 can supply emission reductions generated up to December 2020 into the CORSIA scheme. Within these eligibility requirements, 15 of ADB's DMCs have Clean Development Mechanism project portfolios that qualify for supplying carbon offsets to the pilot phase.

While the eligible carbon credits for the first voluntary period of CORSIA come from projects already initiated, the use of carbon credits generated post-2020 in future CORSIA periods must comply with the rules and guidance established for avoiding double-counting under the Paris Agreement. It is the intention under CORSIA to allow the use of emission units generated from mechanisms under the United Nations Framework Convention on Climate Change (UNFCCC), provided that they align with the ICAO eligibility criteria. However, the lack of agreement on the rulebook for Article 6 of the Paris Agreement, in which new approaches and mechanisms under the UNFCCC are to be elaborated, is a source of uncertainty for the future periods.

ADB has been supporting its DMCs through its ongoing Carbon Market Program on the development and use of market mechanisms and will continue to play a leadership role in the development of post-2020 carbon markets. As part of these efforts, ADB strives to contribute to knowledge and capacity building to encourage deeper understanding of the ongoing international discussions and technical options available for the development and implementation of international carbon markets, including CORSIA.

ADB hopes that this publication will be useful to climate policy makers and carbon offset suppliers in DMCs in building an in-depth understanding of the challenges and opportunities that are created from the CORSIA scheme. In addition to identifying potential offset-selling prospects, it is hoped that this publication will help DMCs formulate coherent policies to enable them to capitalize on the opportunity to supply carbon offsets to international aviation.

Preety Bhandari
Chief of Climate Change and Disaster Risk
Management Thematic Group and
Director, Climate Change
and Disaster Risk Management Division
Sustainable Development and
Climate Change Department
Asian Development Bank

Virender Kumar Duggal
Principal Climate Change Specialist and
Fund Manager, Future Carbon Fund
Sustainable Development and
Climate Change Department
Asian Development Bank

Acknowledgments

This knowledge product on *Carbon Offsetting in International Aviation in Asia and the Pacific: Challenges and Opportunities,* has been developed by the Article 6 Support Facility under Asian Development Bank's (ADB) Carbon Market Program within its Sustainable Development and Climate Change Department.

Virender Kumar Duggal, principal climate change specialist, Climate Change and Disaster Risk Management Division, ADB, conceptualized and guided development of this knowledge product. Takeshi Miyata, climate change specialist, supported its development.

The knowledge product has been developed with inputs by a team of experts engaged under ADB's ongoing Technical Assistance 9695: Establishing a Support Facility for Article 6 of the Paris Agreement, which included George Anjaparidze and Johan Nylander, whose technical inputs are greatly appreciated. This report also benefited from advice and inputs from Naresh Badhwar, Rastraraj Bhandari, Deborah Cornland, Hannah Ebro, and Sangmi Hanh, which are appreciated.

This knowledge product has hugely benefited from the peer review conducted by the Institute for Global Environmental Strategies, Japan, which is sincerely acknowledged and appreciated.

The timely publication of this report was made possible by the valuable coordination and administrative support of Anna Liza Cinco, Ken Edward Concepcion, Jeanette Morales and Ghia Villareal, and through the diligent inputs from Layla Amar, Lawrence Casiraya, Edith Creus, and Jess Alfonso Macasaet.

Abbreviations

ACR	American Carbon Registry
ADB	Asian Development Bank
CAR	Climate Action Reserve
CDM	Clean Development Mechanism
CER	certified emission reduction
CO_2	carbon dioxide
CORSIA	Carbon Offsetting and Reduction Scheme for International Aviation
COVID-19	coronavirus disease
DMC	developing member country
GHG	greenhouse gas
IATA	International Air Transport Association
ICAO	International Civil Aviation Organization
ITMO	internationally transferred mitigation outcome
NDC	nationally determined contribution
SAF	sustainable aviation fuel
tCO_2e	metric ton of carbon dioxide equivalent
UNFCCC	United Nations Framework Convention on Climate Change
US	United States
VCS	Verified Carbon Standard

Executive Summary

International aviation is the first global sector with an absolute cap on net carbon dioxide (CO_2) emissions. One of the key climate goals agreed by the member states of the International Civil Aviation Organization (ICAO) was to achieve zero net growth in CO_2 emissions from 2020 onward. It was in this context that the Carbon Offsetting and Reduction Scheme for International Aviation (CORSIA) was created. However, in light of the sharp downturn of industry traffic in 2020, the base year for evaluating progress toward the zero net growth target was changed to 2019. According to ICAO, this decision was taken to avoid imposing an "inappropriate economic burden to aeroplane operators." Due to the baseline revision and impact of the coronavirus disease (COVID-19), CORSIA's demand for carbon offsets may be non-existent in the short term. During the CORSIA pilot phase, supply of emission units from already approved mechanisms is likely to outnumber even the most optimistic offset demand forecasts considered in this report by a ratio of about three to one.

Based on scenario analyses undertaken within the scope of this report, post-COVID-19 demand for carbon offsets from CORSIA may be from 1 billion to 2 billion metric tons of carbon dioxide equivalent from 2021 to 2035. This represents a major opportunity for carbon offset suppliers. Furthermore, there will be a significant increase in offset demand if the net CO_2 emission trajectory of the sector is to align with the temperature goals of the Paris Agreement.

The developing member countries (DMCs) of the Asian Development Bank (ADB) are especially well-positioned to supply carbon offset credits to international aviation. They can potentially deliver large-scale emission reductions at relatively low cost. By supplying carbon credits, DMCs can generate financial inflows to support climate-friendly investments, while stimulating technology transfer and creating green jobs.

In contrast, long-term growth of international aviation and demand for carbon offsets look strong. However, there is a high degree of uncertainty about which mechanisms will be allowed in the longer term. Policy makers and private investors can reduce these uncertainties and position DMCs to become CORSIA carbon-offset suppliers by seizing opportunities to overcoming specific challenges.

Opportunities to Overcome Challenges Facing Climate Policy Makers in Developing Member Countries

During the pilot phase, which will last from 2021 to 2023, a key policy challenge is to avoid double counting, especially double claiming of emission reductions. ADB DMC policy makers can better position their carbon offset suppliers for CORSIA by filling the gap in the international rules and proactively putting in place clear policies on how to prevent double counting between national mitigation action, international cooperation, and CORSIA-related credits.

Throughout the lifetime of the program, from 2021 to 2035, the challenge would be to prevent disjointed policies on domestic mitigation and international cooperation. Thus, those who shape climate policies in the participating

DMCs need to ensure that there is coherence as it relates to national climate actions and international cooperation under the Paris Agreement as well as CORSIA.

Another challenge during the lifetime of the program is that some DMCs may lack access to desired mechanisms for generating CORSIA-eligible offsets. This is why there is scope to support policies that make it easier to deploy the approved mechanisms under CORSIA within the respective jurisdictions of the DMCs.

Opportunities to Overcome Challenges Facing Carbon Offset Suppliers in Developing Member Countries

In the pilot phase of the program, there may be little to no demand from CORSIA for credits due to COVID-19 shock. Nevertheless, two-way information exchange initiatives between offset suppliers and airlines can create opportunities for cooperation on voluntary offsetting.

The combination of project-specific risks and higher countrywide risk factors can create an unbearably high-risk perception for implementing projects in developing countries. There is an opportunity to use carbon fund vehicles to manage underperformance risks through project pooling and other risk management techniques, while offering more tailored carbon products for meeting airline needs and securing future revenue streams for offset suppliers in DMCs.

1 Introduction

Participating in international carbon markets offers Asian Development Bank (ADB) developing member countries (DMCs) an opportunity to improve the financing environment for climate-friendly investments that can enable technology transfer and create green jobs. International aviation is expected to be a major buyer of carbon offsets as the sector embarks on meeting industry climate targets. DMCs are particularly well-positioned to benefit from being a source of supply of carbon offsets to international aviation given their relatively low marginal abatement costs.

This report is intended to benefit carbon offset suppliers and national climate policy makers in DMCs by increasing their understanding of emerging challenges and opportunities on the nexus of aviation and climate policy.

1.1 Global Emissions from International Aviation

The aviation sector accounts for approximately 2% of global anthropogenic carbon dioxide (CO_2) emissions, of which about 65% relates to international aviation. The International Civil Aviation Organization (ICAO) estimates that in 2015, international aviation was responsible for emitting about 506 million metric tons of CO_2.[1]

Beyond CO_2 emissions, ICAO recognizes that the Intergovernmental Panel on Climate Change (IPCC) special report on Aviation and the Global Atmosphere identified significant scientific uncertainty on the impact of other aircraft emissions on climate and the ozone layer. In this context, ICAO is committed to updating information contained in the IPCC special report and aims to remain at the forefront of developing methods and tools for quantifying aviation's greenhouse gas (GHG) emissions.[2]

CO_2 emissions from international aviation are expected to double within 18 to 25 years. The ICAO traffic forecast, used by the 11th Committee on Aviation Environmental Protection, projects international aviation traffic to grow at a compound annual growth rate of about 4.4% per year from 2015 to 2035 (Figure 1). ICAO scenarios for estimating the scale of fuel efficiency improvements from technology and operations point to a range of 0.57% to 1.5% improvement in fuel efficiency per year.

Two key developments, which occurred since these forecasts were prepared, could significantly change the industry outlook. The most immediate development has been the onset of coronavirus disease (COVID-19), which has created a major shock to the aviation sector and the global economy. The airline industry is

---

[1] ICAO. 2019. Destination Green: The Next Chapter. *ICAO Environmental Report 2019: Aviation and Environment.* Chapter 1. https://www.icao.int/environmental-protection/Pages/envrep2019.aspx.
[2] ICAO. 2019. Resolution A40-18: Consolidated Statement of Continuing ICAO Policies and Practices Related to Environmental Protection - Climate Change. Assembly 40th Session. Montreal. 24 September to 4 October. https://www.icao.int/Meetings/a40/Documents/Resolutions/a40_res_prov_en.pdf.

experiencing an extreme drop in passenger traffic. Current expectations point to a significant contraction that could impact the industry growth profile up to 2035. The second development relates to a major shift in consumer sentiment as a result of concerns about climate change.

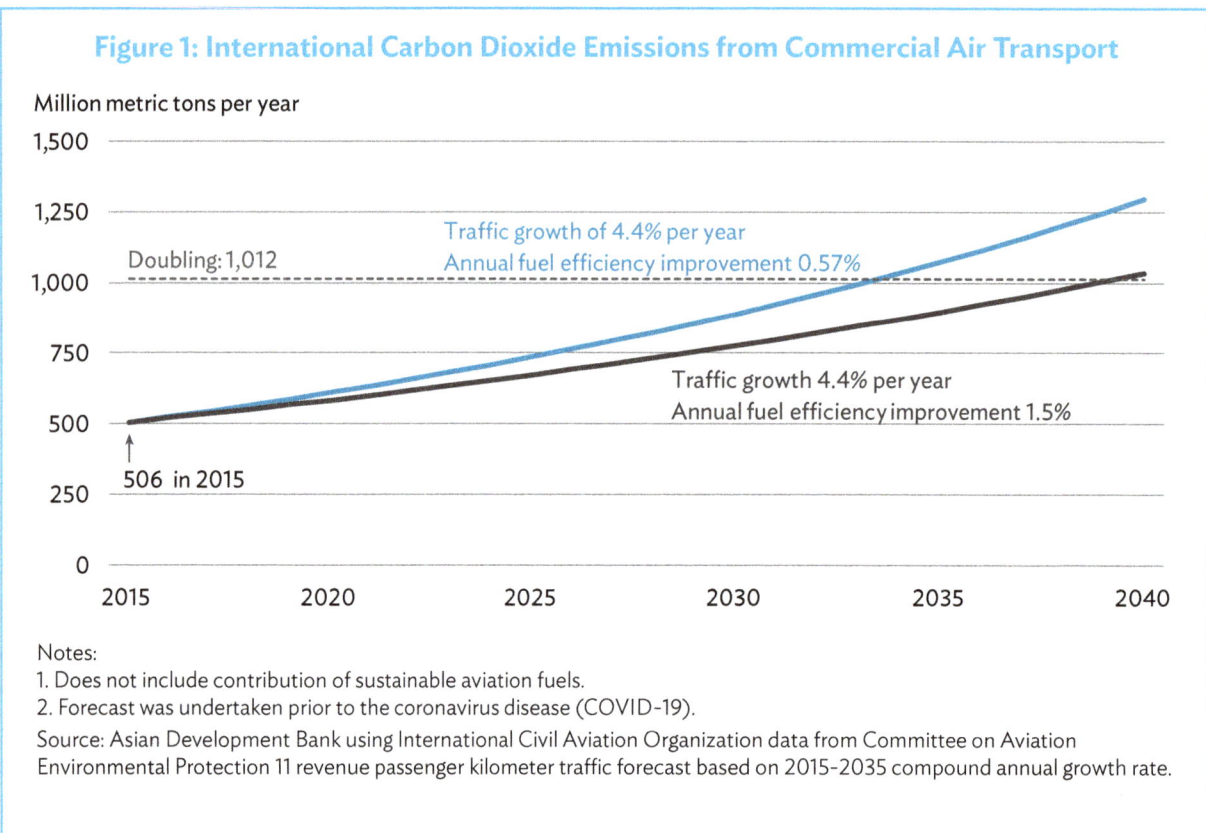

Figure 1: International Carbon Dioxide Emissions from Commercial Air Transport

Notes:
1. Does not include contribution of sustainable aviation fuels.
2. Forecast was undertaken prior to the coronavirus disease (COVID-19).
Source: Asian Development Bank using International Civil Aviation Organization data from Committee on Aviation Environmental Protection 11 revenue passenger kilometer traffic forecast based on 2015-2035 compound annual growth rate.

1.2 Climate Policy for International Aviation

Multilateral climate cooperation between governments is negotiated under the United Nations Framework Convention on Climate Change (UNFCCC). However, emissions associated with international transportation (aviation and maritime) have been negotiated at respective specialized agencies of the UN, specifically ICAO and the International Maritime Organization.[3] These agencies periodically report on their progress in addressing climate change to the UNFCCC through the Subsidiary Body on Scientific and Technological Advice.[4]

Governments signed the Convention on International Civil Aviation (also known as the Chicago Convention) in 1944 to help international civil aviation develop in a safe and orderly manner. A key overarching principle was to establish international air services on the basis of equality of opportunity and operate them soundly and economically. ICAO is an international governmental organization that was established to govern and administer the Chicago Convention. The International Air Transport Association (IATA) is a business association that was

---

[3] There have been discussions within the UNFCCC under the theme of "bunker fuels." For example, Article 2.2 of the Kyoto Protocol calls on some Parties to advance the work on limiting or reducing GHG emissions through ICAO and the International Maritime Organization. UNFCCC. 1997. Kyoto Protocol to the United Nations Framework Convention on Climate Change. Kyoto. 1–10 December. https://unfccc.int/sites/default/files/resource/docs/cop3/l07a01.pdf.

[4] Emissions from domestic air transport are not part of ICAO discussions. These, as well as other domestic sources of GHG emissions, are addressed under the UNFCCC and included in national GHG inventories.

established nearly the same time as the signing of the Chicago Convention. IATA is the prime vehicle for inter-airline cooperation in promoting safe, reliable, secure, and economical air services.

Aviation industry practice is such that standard setting and policy development concerning airline operations are usually first developed by IATA and subsequently adopted by governments through ICAO. Although IATA does not have a decision-making role within ICAO processes, there is a close working relationship and IATA expertise is actively sought out when developing ICAO policies and standards. The airline industry played a key role in framing and designing the current climate change policies adopted by ICAO.[5]

Resolutions adopted by ICAO related to climate change detail a series of measures and activities that aim to achieve two global aspirational goals:

- a 2% annual fuel efficiency improvement until 2050[6] and
- net carbon-neutral growth from 2020 (in practice 2019) onward.[7]

The above goals are envisioned to be achieved through a set of measures, including aircraft technology improvements, sustainable aviation fuels, operational improvements, and market-based measures.

In addition to the two existing goals, and in light of the temperature goals enshrined in the Paris Agreement, ICAO is assessing the feasibility of adopting a new long-term global aspirational goal for international aviation. The next ICAO Assembly, scheduled for 2022, is expected to consider options and an implementation road map. ICAO has already noted the collective commitments announced by aviation industry associations to reduce net CO_2 emissions by 50% by 2050 compared to 2005 levels.[8] ICAO may choose to move from simply noting a 2050 net CO_2 emission reduction target to adopting a similar, or perhaps an even more stringent, target in the future.

---

[5] G. Anjaparidze. 2019. The Extraordinary Climate Agreement on International Aviation: An Airline Industry Perspective. *Policy Brief: Harvard Project on Climate Agreements*. October. https://www.belfercenter.org/publication/extraordinary-climate-agreement-international-aviation-airline-industry-perspective.
[6] The aspirational global fuel efficiency improvement rate of 2% per annum is calculated on the basis of volume of fuel used per revenue ton kilometer (RTK) performed.
[7] A 30 June 2020 ICAO Council decision, in practice, focuses industry efforts on achieving net carbon-neutral growth from 2019 onward.
[8] These commitments were announced in 2008. Industry groups may choose to update their targets in light of the latest international policy developments and scientific knowledge.

2 Carbon Offsetting and Reduction Scheme for International Aviation

2.1 Rationale for the Offsetting Scheme

ICAO member states have agreed to achieve the aviation sector's climate goals through a set of measures, including aircraft technology improvements, sustainable aviation fuels, operational improvements, and market-based measures. Within market-based measures, a carbon offsetting scheme was deemed to be the most appropriate because of its potential to contribute to achieving defined goals cost-effectively (by tapping into abatement potential in other sectors), while being relatively simple to administer. Beyond fleet renewal and improvements in load factors, aviation has high CO_2 abatement costs. There is some scope to achieve negative cost abatement through improvements in air-navigation services and airline operations (Figure 2). However, there are non-price barriers to realizing these opportunities. Over the next decade, cost-effective measures within the aviation sector can deliver about 20% of the CO_2 emission reductions needed to achieve the target of carbon-neutral growth from 2019.[9] The cheapest positive cost abatement measures within the aviation sector (engine retrofits or upgrades and early retirement of planes) cost about $200 per metric ton of CO_2.

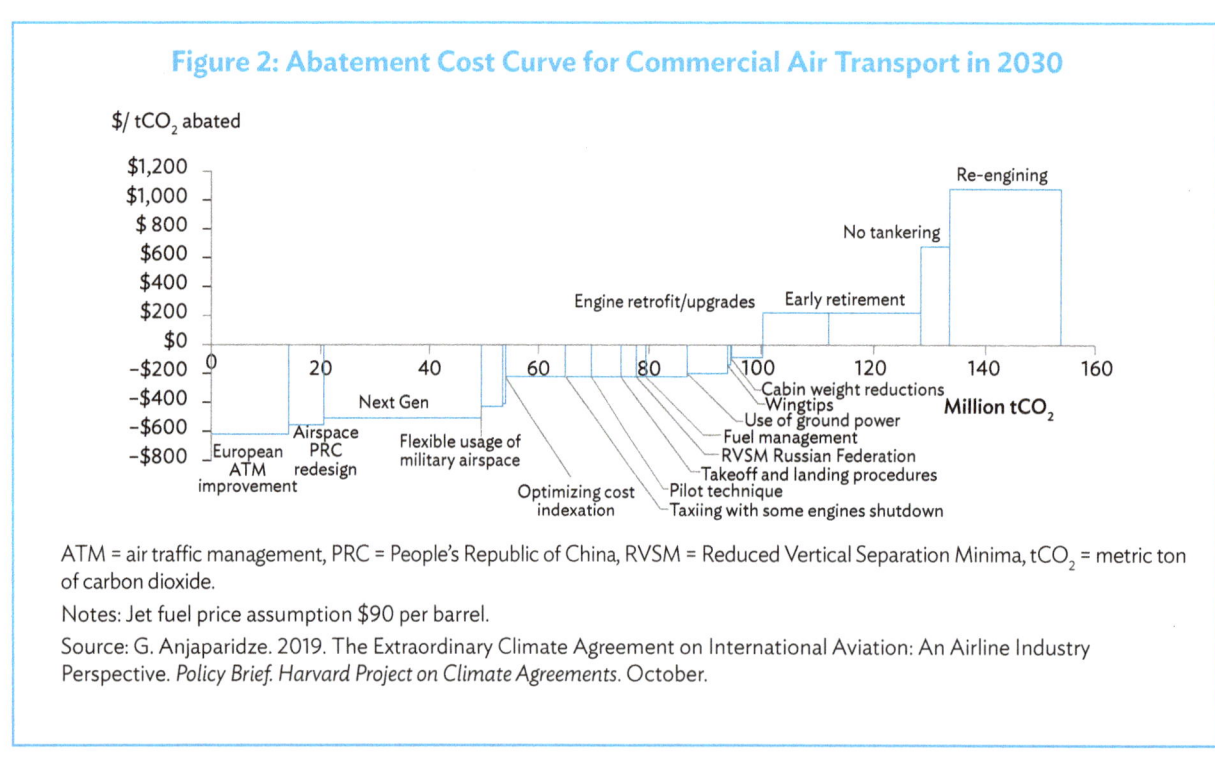

Figure 2: Abatement Cost Curve for Commercial Air Transport in 2030

ATM = air traffic management, PRC = People's Republic of China, RVSM = Reduced Vertical Separation Minima, tCO_2 = metric ton of carbon dioxide.
Notes: Jet fuel price assumption $90 per barrel.
Source: G. Anjaparidze. 2019. The Extraordinary Climate Agreement on International Aviation: An Airline Industry Perspective. *Policy Brief. Harvard Project on Climate Agreements.* October.

---

[9] G. Anjaparidze. 2019. Change of CORSIA. *Airline Routes & Ground Services Magazine.* Winter 2019. p. 44. https://airlinergs.com/issue/winter-2019/.

2.2 Design of the Scheme

The Carbon Offsetting and Reduction Scheme for International Aviation (CORSIA) is a carbon offsetting scheme that addresses the growth in total CO_2 emissions from international aviation. When the scheme was adopted in 2016, the average CO_2 emissions in 2019 and 2020 was set as the baseline above which zero-net-growth in CO_2 emissions was to be achieved. However, in June 2020 the ICAO Council decided that only 2019 emissions would be used as the baseline for the pilot phase (2021 to 2023) considering that the inclusion of 2020 emissions would create an inappropriate economic burden on aeroplane operators.[10] Excluding 2020 CO_2 emissions from the baseline will lead to a higher baseline as the industry experienced a sharp downturn in 2020 due to the onset of the coronavirus disease. Prior to the ICAO Council decision, the airline industry was reported to be concerned that in the absence of the baseline revision, countries may reconsider or avoid joining CORSIA given the higher than expected cost burden.[11] The communication from the ICAO secretariat announcing the Council decision also stressed that the upcoming periodic review of CORSIA, beginning in 2022, would consider other possible adjustments. Given this uncertainty and the extraordinary circumstances observed in 2020, this report extends the use of 2019 CO_2 emissions as the basis for estimating the baseline over the lifetime of the scheme.

There are three key design elements of CORSIA (Figure 3): (i) a formula for allocating offset responsibility, (ii) a phased approach to implementation, and (iii) provisions related to scheme application. The scheme is subject to periodic review and is also underpinned by a process for monitoring, reporting, and verification of CO_2 emissions from international aviation, covering all ICAO member states.

Each airline needs to offset a proportion of its total CO_2 emissions covered by CORSIA on the basis of an industry growth factor above the 2019 industry baseline. Offset responsibilities are allocated to airlines based on this approach. In later years of the scheme (2030–2035), offset responsibilities for individual airlines will be determined through a combination of the sector CO_2 growth rate above the 2019 industry baseline and each individual airline's CO_2 growth rate above their own 2019 baselines.

There are three CORSIA phases. The pilot phase (2021–2023) and first phase (2024–2026) are voluntary. The second phase (2027–2035) is mandatory for all ICAO member states except least-developed countries, small island developing states, landlocked developing countries, and states that represent a very small share of international aviation.[12] By the second phase, CORSIA is envisioned to cover states that represent at least 90% of total international aviation activity.[13] To limit the administrative burden of the scheme, there are some finite technical exemptions for aircraft operators.

---

[10] ICAO. 2020. ICAO Council agrees to safeguard adjustment for CORSIA in light of COVID-19 pandemic. 30 June. https://www.icao.int/Newsroom/Pages/ICAO-Council-agrees-to-the-safeguard-adjustment-for-CORSIA-in-light-of-COVID19-pandemic.aspx.

[11] GreenAir. 2020. IATA calls for change in CORSIA baseline to protect airlines from future higher offsetting requirements. 3 April. https://www.greenaironline.com/news.php?viewStory=2685.

[12] Some states have filed reservations (in full or in part) to ICAO resolutions related to climate change. Reservations allow a state to exclude the legal effect of a specific provision. In addition, ICAO allows states to depart from international standards and procedures by giving notice to the council. Outside of listed exemptions, the second phase applies to all states that have an individual share of international aviation activities in RTKs in the year 2018 above 0.5% of total RTKs, or whose cumulative share in the list of states from the highest to the lowest amount of RTKs reach 90% of total RTKs.

[13] However, if only states representing 90% of RTKs are covered, the percentage of CO_2 emissions covered by the scheme would be considerably below 90%. This is because the exemptions would extend to all flights performed to and from exempt states and not only to the airlines registered there.

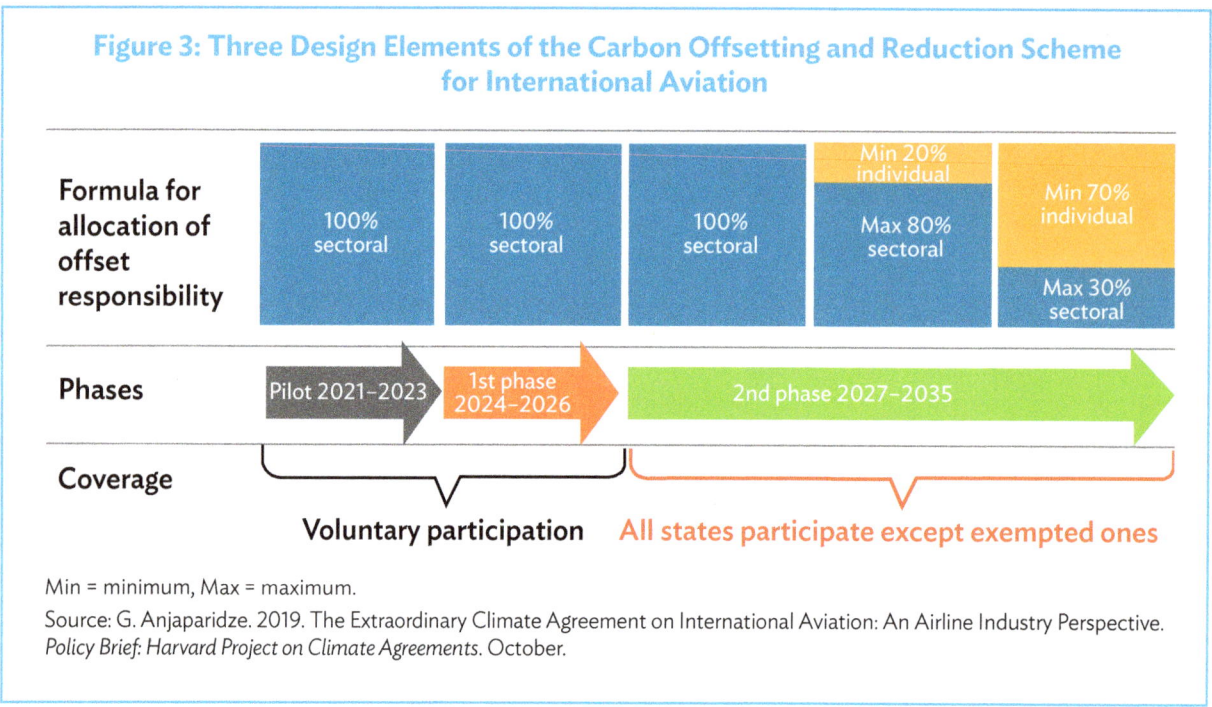

Figure 3: Three Design Elements of the Carbon Offsetting and Reduction Scheme for International Aviation

Min = minimum, Max = maximum.
Source: G. Anjaparidze. 2019. The Extraordinary Climate Agreement on International Aviation: An Airline Industry Perspective. *Policy Brief: Harvard Project on Climate Agreements*. October.

2.3 Scheme Administration and Transparency

The scheme is administered by member states, with data aggregated at the international level by ICAO. The procedures and methods for monitoring, reporting, and verification have been developed through ICAO processes, and have been adopted by ICAO as Standards and Recommended Practices.[14] Under these guidelines, there are two processes for generating data through the monitoring, reporting, and verification system. One process relates to CO_2 emissions while the other relates to emission unit cancellations.

Monitoring, reporting, and verification of carbon dioxide emissions. Aircraft operators are required to monitor and document their CO_2 emissions. In the context of CORSIA, airline operators started monitoring their emissions on 1 January 2019. Following third-party verification, aircraft operators and the verifying entity submit emissions information to the state in which the aircraft operator is registered. The states submit reports to ICAO for determining the Sector Growth Factor above the 2019 industry baseline. The reports are verified during the reporting process: internally by the aircraft operator, by a third-party verifier, and by the relevant state aviation authority.

Monitoring, reporting, and verification of emission unit cancellations. The ICAO estimate of the Sector Growth Factor is used by member states as an input when determining the offset requirements for each aircraft operator within the relevant 3-year compliance period.[15] Aircraft operators are obliged to meet their offsetting requirements by canceling a corresponding quantity of CORSIA-eligible emission units. Following third-party verification, aircraft operators and the verifying entity submit emission unit cancellation information to the designated state. States submit reports to ICAO for aggregation. As in the case of emissions data, reports are

---

[14] ICAO. 2018. Annex 16: Environmental Protection, Volume IV: Carbon Offsetting and Reduction Scheme for International Aviation. 27 June. https://www.icao.int/environmental-protection/CORSIA/Pages/SARPs-Annex-16-Volume-IV.aspx.

[15] If the aircraft operator's total final offsetting requirements during a compliance period is negative, then the aircraft operator has no offsetting requirement for the period. Negative offset requirements shall not be carried forward to subsequent compliance periods.

verified during the process: internally by the aircraft operator, by a third-party verifier, and by the relevant state aviation authority.

A CORSIA Central Registry exists to facilitate the exchange of information and data for implementation and transparency. Existing elements tracked by the Central Registry include

(i) which state each aircraft operator is attributed to,
(ii) total international aviation CO_2 emissions,
(iii) sector growth factors for given years, and
(iv) names of accredited verification bodies in each state.

Further, each of the emission unit programs' registries are considered a relevant designated registry for making information available to the public on CORSIA-eligible emission units that have been cancelled by aircraft operators.

2.4 Criteria for Determining the Eligibility of Emission Units

In March 2019, the ICAO Council adopted emissions unit eligibility criteria for approving mechanisms as supply sources for CORSIA emissions offsets.[16] The adopted criteria incorporate some of the broader elements identified in the guiding principles for the design and implementation of market-based measures for international aviation.[17] The criteria are used to screen the extent to which processes within offset programs address desired design elements. Therefore, a review applying ICAO criteria is not based on a specific technical standard. Rather, it is centered on a procedural demonstration that the offset program has processes in place to address identified concerns.

For example, one of the eligibility criteria are for programs to have clear methodologies and protocols, and processes for developing them. Specifically, the criteria indicate that, "Programs should have qualification and quantification methodologies and protocols in place and available for use as well as a process for developing further methodologies and protocols. The existing methodologies and protocols as well as the process for developing further methodologies and protocols should be publicly disclosed" (footnote 16). This criterion does not require a specific technical standard for methodologies or protocols to be met but, rather, requires that the program demonstrates that it has the identified processes in place.

Some of the assessment criteria contain requirements that are more technical in nature, particularly in the context of assessing identification and tracking requirements as well as the additionality of mitigation activities. The criteria require that additionality is demonstrated using one of several analytical methods, including: barrier analysis; common practice and/or market penetration analysis; investment, cost, or other financial analysis; performance standards or benchmarks; or specific legal or regulatory additionality analysis. In cases when these methods are not identified, there is the option of assessing the evaluation framework based on expert review. While the identified approaches represent technical methods, the actual review of their deployment is still process-centric in nature.

---

[16] ICAO. 2019. CORSIA *Emissions Unit Eligibility Criteria*. March. https://www.icao.int/environmental-protection/CORSIA/Documents/ICAO_Document_09.pdf.

[17] ICAO. 2019. Annex to Resolution A40-18: Consolidated Statement of Continuing ICAO Policies and Practices Related to Environmental Protection - Climate Change. Assembly 40th Session. Montreal. 24 September to 4 October. https://www.icao.int/Meetings/a40/Documents/Resolutions/a40_res_prov_en.pdf.

Assessments of the eligibility of emission units are undertaken at the program level. Assessments are comprised of 11 program design elements and 8 carbon offset credit integrity assessment criteria. Assessment of program design elements includes a focus on ensuring that procedures and processes exist within programs to ensure a technical review of methodologies, transparency in accounting, and the existence of public disclosure practices. The carbon offset credit integrity assessment criteria are used to evaluate whether offset credit programs have processes in place to deliver emission reductions, avoidance, and sequestration, which fit broad characteristics of being additional, credible, quantifiable, transparent, and permanent; and that avoid double counting and leakage as well as do no net harm.

Appendix 1 provides more detailed information on the program design elements and the carbon offset credit integrity assessment criteria.

3 Offset Supply Outlook for International Aviation

3.1 Paris Agreement and Offset Supply Outlook in All Phases, 2021–2035

There is a high degree of uncertainty on which offset mechanisms will be approved for CORSIA supply after the pilot phase. A major source of ambiguity is a lack of agreement on the rules for international cooperation under the Paris Agreement, specifically the negotiations under Article 6. Most important is the need for clear rules to ensure the avoidance of unintended double counting of emission reductions (Box 1). Since CORSIA is working with an open design, risks related to double counting, in general—and double claiming, in particular—need to be addressed. Double issuance and double use are risks that can likely be managed through the registry systems of approved programs. Double claiming of emission reductions is trickier, but for projects where emission reductions are covered by national targets under the Paris framework this could be managed through the accounting framework under Article 6 of the Paris Agreement.

As negotiation texts currently stand for cooperative approaches under Article 6, the accounting provisions under Article 6.2 allow for different programs or mechanisms to be used for offsetting, as long as international transfer of offsets is subject to robust accounting, i.e., corresponding adjustments to avoid double counting. If these provisions are maintained in the final Article 6 decision, there will be a coordinated approach for addressing double-counting concerns for members of the Paris Agreement. Appendix 2 elaborates double-counting provisions under CORSIA as well as the implications of double-counting provisions under the Paris Agreement that are most relevant to CORSIA.

However, there is a lack of clarity regarding how the accounting framework will deal with a situation if a signatory to the Paris Agreement chooses to supply offsets to CORSIA from outside the scope of their nationally determined contribution (NDC). In many countries, NDCs are not economy-wide, with some sectors falling outside their scope. An analysis published in 2016 by the Food and Agriculture Organization of the United Nations on intended NDCs indicates that 14% of developing countries excluded the agriculture and land use, land-use change, and forestry sectors.[18] It is also a fairly common practice for countries to focus their NDCs on specific GHGs, such as methane and CO_2. Whether, and to what extent, CORSIA will source offsets from outside host-country NDCs remains to be seen. Such cases need to be addressed under future accounting frameworks, at least with respect to transparency. Sourcing offsets from outside the Paris Agreement framework may also have unintended consequences, such as encouraging countries to limit the scope of activities included in their NDCs.[19]

---

[18] R. Strohmaier et al. 2016. The Agriculture Sectors in the Intended Nationally Determined Contributions: Analysis. *Environment and Natural Resources Management Working Paper*. No. 62. Rome: FAO. http://www.fao.org/3/a-i5687e.pdf.

[19] Text proposed for a decision on Article 6 during COP25 contained proposed provisions to also require corresponding adjustments for mitigation outcomes from outside the scope of NDCs to address these concerns. However, consensus was not reached on this text. UNFCCC. 2019. Draft Text on Matters relating to Article 6 of the Paris Agreement: Guidance on Cooperative Approaches Referred to in Article 6, Paragraph 2, of the Paris Agreement, Version 3 of 15 December 00:50 hrs. https://unfccc.int/documents/204687.

Box 1: Avoiding Double Counting in the Pilot Phase

The International Civil Aviation Organization (ICAO) process for identifying eligible emissions explicitly addresses the issue of avoiding double-counting. As part of the screening process, mechanisms must provide clear information on how they have addressed double counting, issuance, and claiming in the context of evolving national and international regimes for carbon markets and emissions trading.

To prevent double claiming, eligible programs are required to demonstrate that host countries of emissions reduction activities agree to account for any offset units issued as a result of those activities. This is intended to ensure that double claiming by the airline and the country hosting the emissions reduction activity does not occur.

- **Double issuance**. This occurs if more than one unit is issued for the same emissions reduction. Double issuance may happen as a result of double registration, which occurs if one mitigation project is registered under two or more international crediting schemes.
- **Double use**. This occurs when the same issued unit is used twice.
- **Double claiming**. This occurs if the same emissions reduction is counted twice (e.g., counted toward the climate change mitigation effort of both an airline and the host country of the emissions reduction activity).

The international regulatory framework for carbon markets under the Paris Agreement is yet to be established. This means that the regulatory framework for accounting and avoiding double counting is still under negotiation. Provisions relating to avoiding double counting exist both in Article 6, which enables the emergence of carbon market mechanisms under the Paris Agreement, and Article 4, which is about countries' nationally determined contributions. However, until there is greater clarity on how double counting will be addressed in the rules regulating carbon markets under the Paris Agreement, sourcing offsets generated under Article 6 mechanisms will involve significant risks.[a]

ICAO intended to limit exposure to such risks by only allowing offsets generated from emission reductions that occurred before 31 December 2020 to be used in the Carbon Offsetting and Reduction Scheme for International Aviation (CORSIA) pilot phase. However, some member states have expressed the view that emissions reductions achieved through the Clean Development Mechanism prior to 2021 could also be used to meet emission reduction commitments under the Paris Agreement as well as other mitigation targets. Despite this uncertainty, criteria and guidelines under the ICAO scheme include specific provisions that are intended to avoid double counting.

ICAO guidelines for the use of emission reduction units clearly indicate that for units to be CORSIA eligible they require a host country attestation confirming that the emission units will not be counted toward other mitigation commitments. Further, the verification guidelines requires documenting that cancelled eligible emission units used to meet airplane operators' offsetting requirements have not been used to offset any other emissions.[b] So long as this verification is global in scope and carried out diligently, the process should safeguard against double counting.

Nevertheless, having clear accounting rules under the Paris Agreement would help to further reduce the risk of double counting of emissions reductions generated from within the Paris framework. In the absence of internationally agreed accounting rules, individual states can provide greater clarity on double-counting considerations by issuing clear policies illuminating how they intend to treat CORSIA-eligible emission reductions.

[a] G. Anjaparidze. 2019. Why is UNFCCC COP25 Important for International Aviation? *International Institute for Sustainable Development*. 3 December. https://sdg.iisd.org/commentary/guest-articles/why-is-unfccc-cop-25-important-for-international-aviation/.
[b] ICAO. 2018. Doc 9501: *Environmental Technical Manual. Volume III—Procedures for the CO_2 Emissions Certification of Aeroplanes*. Montreal. https://www.icao.int/environmental-protection/Documents/Doc_9501_ETM_Vol_III_SGAR%202017.pdf.

Source: Asian Development Bank.

Under the pilot phase, two of the six eligible carbon offsetting programs primarily source carbon offsets from outside Paris Agreement jurisdictions. The American Carbon Registry (ACR) and Climate Action Reserve (CAR) predominantly generate carbon offsets from projects in the United States (US).[20] From a purely technical perspective, using offsets generated from these programs in the pilot phase and subsequent CORSIA compliance periods avoids unintended double counting of emission reduction under the Paris Agreement. However, it raises other concerns on the political appropriateness of sourcing offsets from jurisdictions and mechanisms that are outside of the Paris Agreement.

Judging from the approach employed in assessing mechanisms for the pilot phase, ICAO is likely to continue to expand the pool of programs that can supply offsets to meet CORSIA demand. Allowing member states more flexibility through which to comply with CORSIA offset requirements may increase the political acceptability of the scheme and can potentially reduce CORSIA compliance costs.

It also remains to be seen whether ICAO's approach to approving offset mechanisms could be compatible with promoting economy-wide cooperative approaches for generating internationally transferred mitigation outcomes that could potentially be used for CORSIA compliance.

3.2 Offset Supply Outlook in the Pilot Phase, 2021–2023

ICAO approved six programs as eligible for generating emissions units that can be used for CORSIA compliance during the pilot phase. The programs were selected following a screening based on emission unit eligibility criteria. In addition to mechanism-specific conditions, ICAO has indicated that, within the approved mechanisms, only units from activities that started their first crediting period on or after 1 January 2016 are eligible.[21] Further, only emission reductions that occurred on or before 31 December 2020 would be allowed. However, aircraft operators have until 31 January 2025 to submit reports confirming that they have cancelled the emission units necessary for compliance under the pilot phase. Therefore, the analysis in this report assumes that credits issued up to 2025 from eligible projects and eligible offset types may be used for compliance within the pilot phase (Figure 4).

---

[20] The United States (US) announced its withdrawal from the Paris Agreement, which, when implemented, would lead its NDC to lose relevance and effectively eliminate the risk of double counting against the NDC. However, if the US were to re-enter the Paris Agreement, eligible carbon offsets sourced from the US for CORSIA compliance would need to demonstrate that they also address double-counting concerns related to the NDC of the US.

[21] As per the crediting period start date specified at the time of registration.

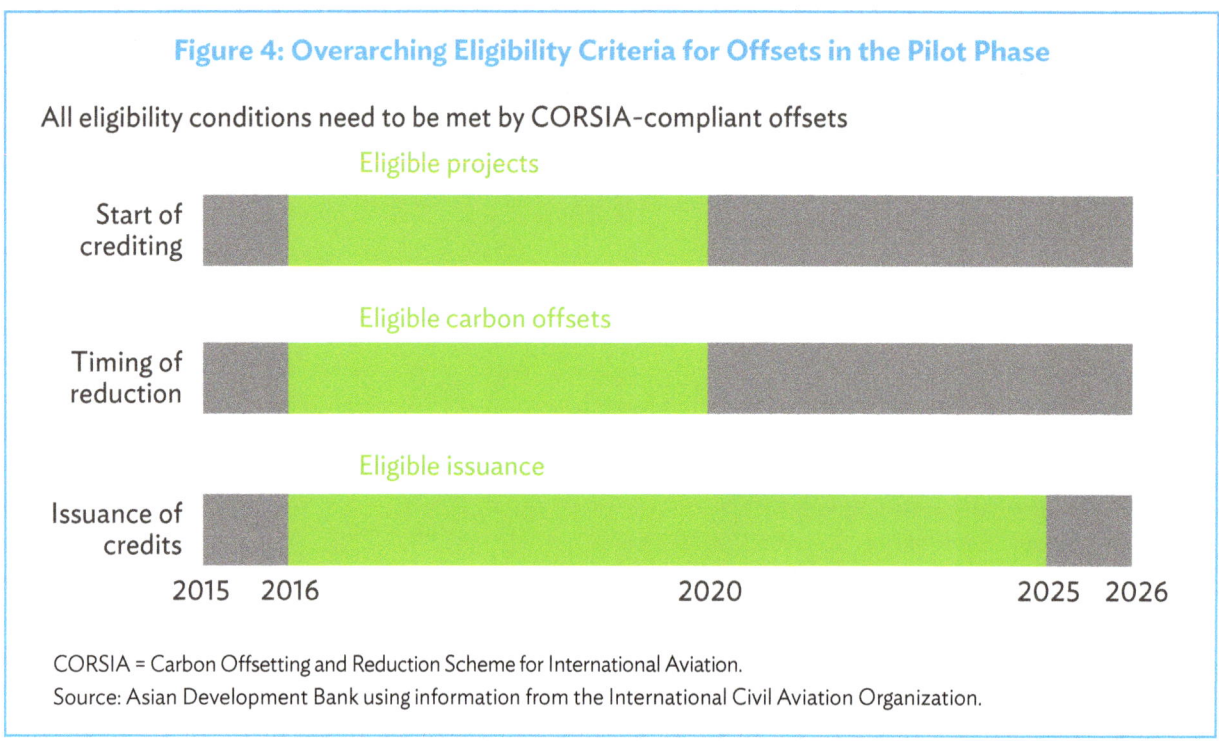

Figure 4: Overarching Eligibility Criteria for Offsets in the Pilot Phase

CORSIA = Carbon Offsetting and Reduction Scheme for International Aviation.
Source: Asian Development Bank using information from the International Civil Aviation Organization.

The approved programs and their brief descriptions are as follows:

- **American Carbon Registry**. ACR issues offsets for voluntary and compliance markets, specifically for use in the California cap-and-trade program. To date, 100% of credits issued from CORSIA-eligible ACR projects have originated from the US.

- **China Greenhouse Gas Voluntary Emission Reduction Program**. This program issues offsets for voluntary and compliance markets, with significant overlap with the Clean Development Mechanism (CDM). All CORSIA-eligible credits issued from this program seem to stem from projects in the People's Republic of China.

- **Clean Development Mechanism**. The CDM issues offsets for compliance markets with optional use for voluntary retirement. To date, 63% of credits issued from CORSIA-eligible CDM projects have originated from ADB developing member countries (DMCs).[22]

- **Climate Action Reserve**. CAR issues offsets for voluntary and compliance markets, specifically for use in the California cap-and-trade program, and serves as its Offset Project Registry. Credits issued by CAR from CORSIA-eligible projects have originated almost exclusively (99.7%) from the US.

- **Gold Standard**. The Gold Standard issues offsets for voluntary markets and quality control labels (focused on environmental integrity and contributions to sustainable development) for offsets issued from the CDM and other offsetting mechanisms. The Gold Standard is primarily focused on projects hosted by developing countries.

- **Verified Carbon Standard**. The Verified Carbon Standard (VCS) issues offsets for the voluntary markets. It develops projects in both developed and developing countries.

---

[22] The CDM's approach to temporary crediting for emissions reductions from afforestation and reforestation activities was found to be incompatible with CORSIA permanence criteria for eligible units. Therefore, afforestation and reforestation activities under the CDM are not eligible to generate CORSIA-compliant offsets. However, other programs that incorporate design features such as buffer pools have been able to successfully address CORSIA's permanence concerns and are qualified to generate CORSIA-eligible units from forestry and afforestation activities.

The aviation sector is not the only source of demand for credits from projects registered under these mechanisms. Nevertheless, as highlighted in Figure 5, the available supply of offsets from these mechanisms is likely to significantly exceed CORSIA demand in the pilot phase. Further, ICAO continues to consider additional mechanisms for sourcing offsets for the pilot phase. As of June 2020, eight additional programs were undergoing review.

Eligible ACR projects are expected to generate offsets representing 43 million metric tons of CO_2 equivalent (tCO_2e) and 20 million tCO_2e from eligible CAR projects.[23] The CDM supply depicted in Figure 5 is based on a conservative estimate of eligible deliveries of credits.[24] To avoid double counting, VCS and Gold Standard issuances were grouped together and only issuances of Verified Emission Reductions were considered in the analysis, which is based on historical processing volumes of these mechanisms. Unfortunately, it was not feasible to estimate the scale of supply that could be delivered by the China GHG Voluntary Emission Reduction Program. Since its inception in 2012, over 43 million tCO_2e in emission reductions have been approved.[25] However, information on the number of CORSIA-eligible projects and the extent to which these overlap with other mechanisms such as the CDM or VCS are not currently possible to assess.

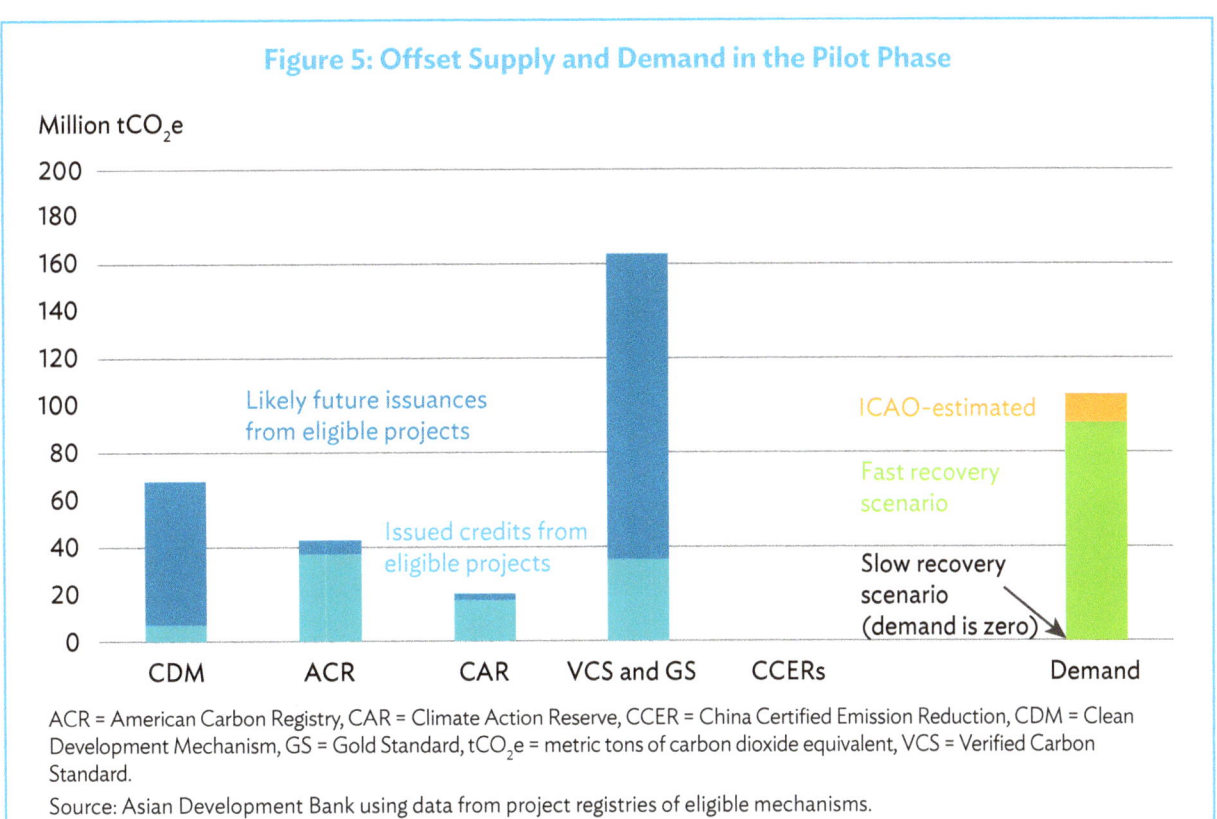

Figure 5: Offset Supply and Demand in the Pilot Phase

ACR = American Carbon Registry, CAR = Climate Action Reserve, CCER = China Certified Emission Reduction, CDM = Clean Development Mechanism, GS = Gold Standard, tCO_2e = metric tons of carbon dioxide equivalent, VCS = Verified Carbon Standard.
Source: Asian Development Bank using data from project registries of eligible mechanisms.

---

[23] Future eligible issuances under ACR and CAR were estimated in proportion to the average issuance observed over a comparable period since 2016. Given the tight time frame between project registration and credit issuance, this assessment assumed an issuance cut off in December 2020.
[24] Details on the methodology used in calculating CDM supply are explained later in this section on pages 14 and 15 of the report.
[25] T. Qing. 2018. Introduction on China Certified Emission Reductions. Presentation during the ICAO Seminar on Carbon Markets. Montreal, Canada. 7 Feb. https://www.icao.int/Meetings/carbonmarkets/Documents/01_Session2_Qing_CCER.pdf.

A total of 15 DMCs have CDM project portfolios that qualify to supply carbon offsets for the pilot phase. Table 1 provides an overview of certified emissions reductions (CERs) issued, and potential delivery volumes, from eligible CDM projects in DMCs.[26]

Table 1 does not reflect potential emission reductions that can be generated from programs of activities that started their first crediting period prior to January 2016.[27]

Table 1: Clean Development Mechanism Supply of Offsets Compliant to the Carbon Offsetting and Reduction Scheme for International Aviation in the Pilot Phase
(million tCO_2e)

Country	Eligible CERs issued	Adjusted CER pipeline	Registered CER pipeline
Bangladesh	3.4	23.5	60.2
India	0.4	8.0	30.3
Indonesia	0.0	0.3	14.2
China, People's Republic of	0.0	0.6	9.0
Viet Nam	0.0	1.1	6.4
Bhutan	0.0	1.9	4.8
Lao People's Democratic Republic	0.1	1.4	3.7
Georgia	0.3	0.5	3.3
Myanmar	0.0	0.9	2.0
Pakistan	0.3	0.7	1.8
Philippines	0.0	0.0	0.9
Sri Lanka	0.0	0.1	0.3
Korea, Republic of	0.0	0.0	0.1
Thailand	0.0	0.0	0.0
Cambodia	0.0	0.0	0.0
DMC total	**4.6**	**39.1**	**137.0**
DMC as % of developing country total	63%	58%	58%
Developing country total (global)	**7.2**	**67.1**	**237.2**

CDM = Clean Development Mechanism, CER = certified emission reduction, DMC = developing member country, tCO_2e = metric ton of carbon dioxide equivalent, UNFCCC = United Nations Framework Convention on Climate Change.
Note: Countries are listed in descending order (largest to smallest) by volume of eligible CERs registered in the CDM pipeline.
Source: Asian Development Bank using data from the UNFCCC Secretariat (updated April 2020).

Globally, by 31 December 2020, the total volume of offsets in the pipeline from registered CDM projects that are CORSIA-eligible could be as large as 237 million CERs (237 million tCO_2e in emission reductions).[28]

However, some CERs in the pipeline are from "ghost" projects that have faced project implementation challenges and/or have abandoned administrative processes leading to CER issuances. A conservative assessment, based on filtering out potentially problematic projects and applying conservative adjustments to the CER

---

[26] One CER represents emission reductions of 1 tCO_2e.
[27] Emission reductions generated prior to December 2020, from component project activities that started their crediting period after January 2016, could potentially be eligible under the pilot phase, even if they come from programs of activities registered prior to 2016. However, these emission reductions are not included in the assessment presented in this report.
[28] Only CDM projects with a UNFCCC website status of being registered have been considered in the pipeline.

pipeline, is that 67 million tCO$_2$e in emission reductions could be generated from eligible CDM projects through 31 December 2020.[29]

As of April 2020, 7.2 million metric tons of CERs had been issued that were CORSIA-eligible. Adjusting for credits that have been reported as retired, about 7 million metric tons of CERs already exist and may be available for immediate use. Credit issuance from eligible CDM projects is expected to surge as more projects enter the credit issuance stage of the CDM project cycle.[30] Figure 6 offers a visual representation of global CORSIA-eligible CERs supply for the pilot phase.

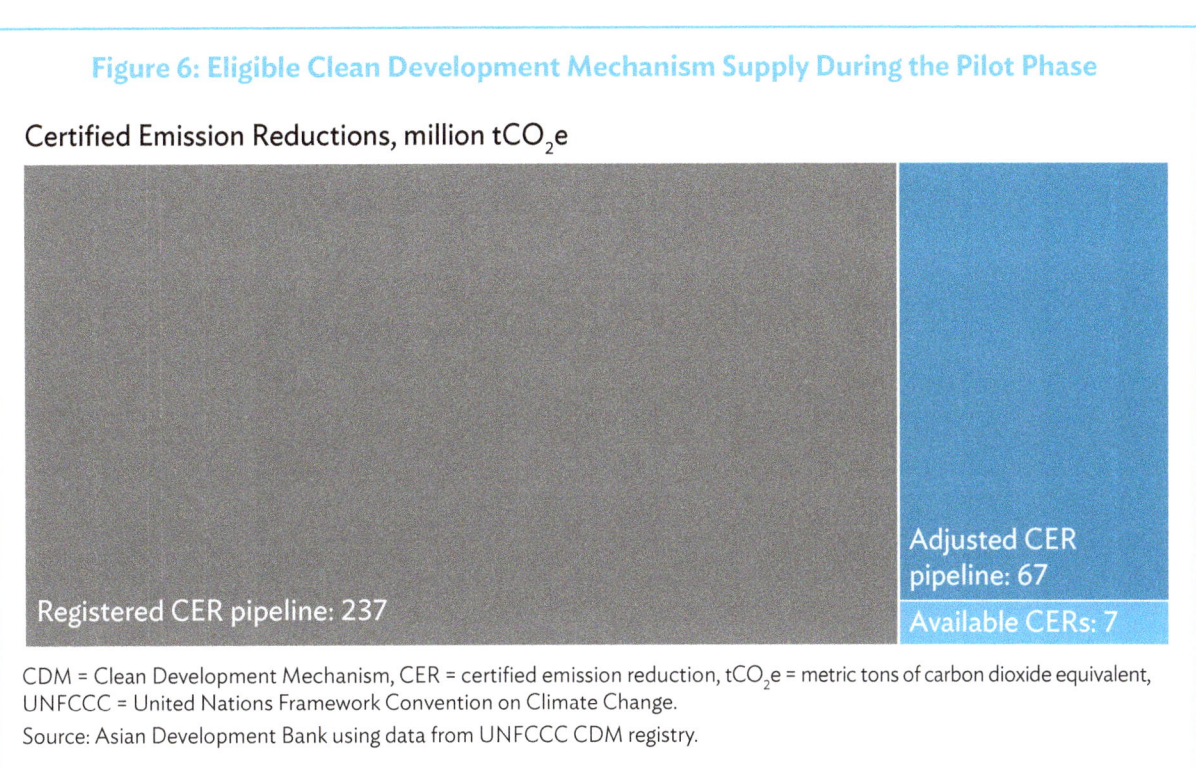

Figure 6: Eligible Clean Development Mechanism Supply During the Pilot Phase

Certified Emission Reductions, million tCO$_2$e

Registered CER pipeline: 237
Adjusted CER pipeline: 67
Available CERs: 7

CDM = Clean Development Mechanism, CER = certified emission reduction, tCO$_2$e = metric tons of carbon dioxide equivalent, UNFCCC = United Nations Framework Convention on Climate Change.
Source: Asian Development Bank using data from UNFCCC CDM registry.

---

[29] A CER pipeline filter, based on whether CDM projects have had recent communication with the UNFCCC Secretariat (i.e., since 2016) and have been assigned a chronological number as a registered CDM activity, was used as a proxy for screening out deserted projects. In addition, to also account for under-delivery of emission reductions (lower than the volumes predicted upon registration), a further downward adjustment of 61% has been applied to arrive at a conservative share of the CER pipeline that is likely to result in issuance within the desired time frame. The 61% downward adjustment is based on the ratio of observed issuances in 2016–2020 compared to anticipated emission reductions that were identified in the 2013–2015 CER pipeline, calculated for a 4-year period.

[30] The estimated quantity of potential annual emission reductions (the CER pipeline) associated with registered CDM projects accumulates each year, which, by the end of 2020, leads to a significant growth in emission reductions. For a project to be eligible under CORSIA, it needs to have started its crediting period in 2016. These projects are expected to continue to generate emissions reductions every year up through 2020. Emission reductions generated by newly registered projects are additional to the emission reductions generated by projects registered during previous years. Therefore, the cumulative impact translates to continued growth in the annual emissions reductions generated in 2020 from the starting point of 2016.

4 Demand Outlook for Offsets by International Aviation and Impact of COVID-19

4.1 The Impact of COVID-19 on International Aviation Traffic

The coronavirus disease (COVID-19) has led to the largest prolonged fall in air traffic activity on record. The shock has disrupted air transport networks and created an overall fear of traveling. Globally, governments have imposed an unprecedented scale of travel restrictions and border controls. The short-term impacts of COVID-19 will result in significantly lower air traffic volumes in 2020 compared to recent years. The International Civil Aviation Organization (ICAO) expects seat capacity offered by airlines in 2020 to be 33% to 60% lower than business as usual.[31] The International Air Transport Association (IATA) has estimated a 48% fall in passenger traffic in 2020 compared to 2019.[32] The impacts beyond 2020 are very uncertain.

Over the next 5 years, the pace of the recovery for the aviation industry will depend largely on the COVID-19 epidemiological situation and government restrictions on travel, as well as the general macroeconomic backdrop. The extent of behavioral change at the societal level as a lingering result of COVID-19 responses may also be a contributing factor influencing the pace of the recovery. IATA expects passenger traffic in 2021 to be 32% to 41% below the pre-COVID-19 historic growth trend, with international travel being even more adversely impacted. For 2025, IATA expects passenger air traffic to be 10% below the levels that would have been observed under their pre-COVID-19 scenario.[33] However, assuming that behavioral changes in response to COVID-19 do not become permanent, growth could rebound more quickly if the threat from the virus subsides sooner than expected, and the travel and tourism industry implements measures that increases the confidence of governments and travelers.

In the long term, over the next 20 years and beyond, demand for air transport is likely to be constrained by concerns related to climate change (due to the perception that air transport is unsustainable). Flight-shaming movements have grown in momentum. Just prior to the COVID-19 outbreak, the aviation industry was experiencing a drastic and immediate shift in stated consumer sentiment as a result of concerns related to climate change. A survey by the European Investment Bank conducted at the end of 2019 found that 76% of Europeans, 94% of Chinese, and 69% of Americans intended to fly less for holidays in 2020 as a way to help in the fight against climate change.[34] The same survey identified that only about 36% of European respondents had

---

[31] ICAO. 2020. *Effects of Novel Coronavirus on Civil Aviation: Economic Impact Analysis*. 25 May. https://www.icao.int/sustainability/Documents/COVID-19/ICAO%20COVID%202020%2005%2025%20Economic%20Impact.pdf.
[32] IATA. 2020. *COVID-19 Updated Impact Assessment*. 14 April. https://www.iata.org/en/iata-repository/publications/economic-reports/covid-fourth-impact-assessment/.
[33] IATA. 2020. *COVID-19 Outlook for Air Travel in the Next 5 Years*. 13 May. https://www.iata.org/en/iata-repository/publications/economic-reports/covid-19-outlook-for-air-travel-in-the-next-5-years/.
[34] European Investment Bank (EIB). 2020. 2nd EIB Climate Survey: Citizens' Commitment to Fight Climate Change in 2020. https://www.eib.org/en/surveys/2nd-citizen-survey/new-years-resolutions.htm.

reduced their air travel in 2019 for climate change reasons. If stated preferences are acted on when making travel-related decisions, demand for air travel will suffer.[35] However, loss of demand due to sustainability concerns could potentially be restored if the industry successfully responds to growing climate concerns by scaling up climate action and revamping its sustainability credentials.

Figure 7 presents two consolidated scenarios for trajectories of CO_2 emissions from international air transport after the onset of COVID-19. Both scenarios are modeled based on the assumption that international traffic falls by 48% in 2020 compared to 2019, which is consistent with the range of scenarios presented in the ICAO COVID-19 impact analysis (footnote 31). The scenarios are compared against the ICAO 20-year growth trend forecast, with an embedded annual fuel efficiency improvement of 0.57%.

These two scenarios depict the likely range for CO_2 emissions from international air transport during the 2021-2035 time period. The presented scenarios are also used to highlight how some of the design features of the scheme impact offset demand. Obviously, each of these scenario tracks can generate hundreds of different forecasts with varying parameters. A key downside risk to the presented scenarios is a prolonged delay in international air traffic recovery from the COVID-19 shock. Some industry analysts have predicted that it may take industry even longer to return to pre-COVID-19 levels of traffic then has been suggested by the scenarios presented in this report.

- Under the slow recovery and subdued growth scenario, international aviation recovers gradually, reaching 2019 levels in 2022. From 2023 onward, this scenario adds an adjustment for subdued growth due to consumer concerns related to climate change. Growth is 1.5 percentage points lower than the ICAO 20-year forecast. Under this scenario, carbon dioxide (CO_2) emissions in 2035 would still be about 30% higher than 2019 emissions, assuming continued improvement in fuel efficiency in line with historic performance.

- Under the fast recovery and trend growth scenario, international aviation rebounds to historical trend growth in 2021, consistent with the ICAO 20-year traffic forecast for 2015–2035. Emissions are lower than the ICAO reference scenario, as this scenario assumes continued improvement in fuel efficiency in line with historic performance. In this scenario, the impacts of COVID-19 are confined to 2020 activity. As a result, CO_2 emissions in 2035 would be 61% higher than those in 2019.

The fast recovery scenario is the most optimistic case considered in this report. It could materialize if there is a rapid improvement in the epidemiological situation followed by a boom in air travel activity. The combination of pent-up travel demand and a robust supply side response, as airlines and travel industry actors rush to recapture market share, has the potential to boost air traffic activity. Whether it would be enough to bring the industry back to emission levels consistent with trend growth as early as 2021 remains to be seen and would be highly dependent on the epidemiological situation. However, over the longer term, it is important to keep in mind that the trend in CO_2 emissions modeled under the fast recovery and trend growth scenario may be maintained even under conditions of lower traffic growth, for example, due to worse performance in making improvements on fuel efficiency. Therefore, the fast recovery with trend growth scenario is a relevant scenario to consider for looking at aggregate emissions over the lifetime of the scheme (2021 to 2035) even if the recovery takes longer to materialize.

Under both scenarios, international aviation is expected to experience an upward growth trajectory in CO_2 emissions. The anticipated impact of COVID-19 has placed the aviation industry on an emission trajectory that is temporarily consistent with the temperature goal of 1.5°C of the Paris Agreement.[36] However, even the slow

---

[35] While not all people may act as they say they will, the uptick in climate change concerns suggests weaker demand for air transport.
[36] The 1.5°C consistent trajectory is estimated on the basis of the UNEP 2019 Emissions Gap Report, which quantifies it as 3.3% annual reduction in CO_2 emissions starting from 2010.

recovery and subdued growth scenario leads to continued CO_2 growth from international aviation that will far exceed the limitations needed to remain compatible with the Paris Agreement (Figure 7).

Aviation industry-wide initiatives, and internationally agreed climate policy goals at ICAO, address CO_2 emission growth through a combination of industry-focused climate action and the use of carbon offsets. The aviation industry goal of carbon-neutral growth from 2019 onward, as well as more ambitious targets of aligning net CO_2 emissions with the temperature goals of the Paris Agreement, can be achieved within the existing framework, by increasing the use of carbon offsets.

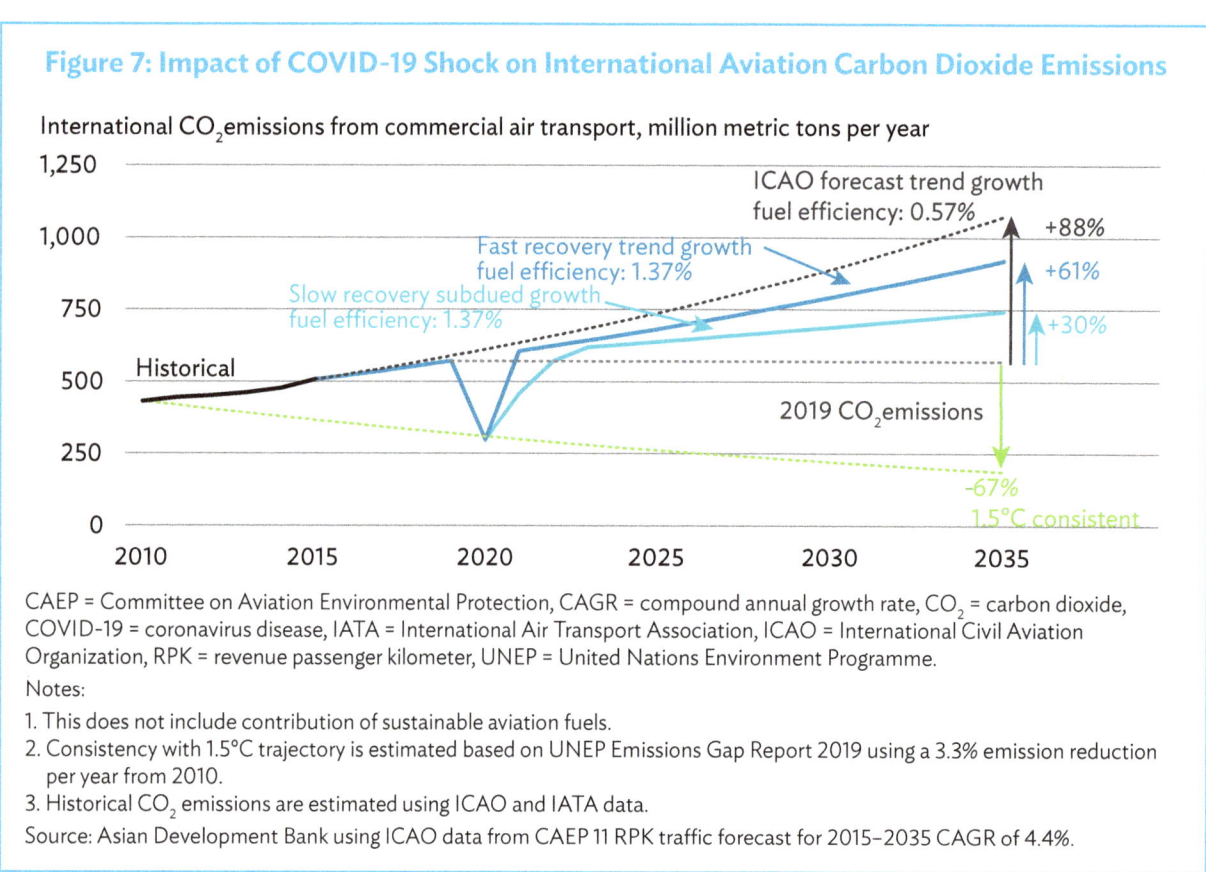

Figure 7: Impact of COVID-19 Shock on International Aviation Carbon Dioxide Emissions

CAEP = Committee on Aviation Environmental Protection, CAGR = compound annual growth rate, CO_2 = carbon dioxide, COVID-19 = coronavirus disease, IATA = International Air Transport Association, ICAO = International Civil Aviation Organization, RPK = revenue passenger kilometer, UNEP = United Nations Environment Programme.
Notes:
1. This does not include contribution of sustainable aviation fuels.
2. Consistency with 1.5°C trajectory is estimated based on UNEP Emissions Gap Report 2019 using a 3.3% emission reduction per year from 2010.
3. Historical CO_2 emissions are estimated using ICAO and IATA data.
Source: Asian Development Bank using ICAO data from CAEP 11 RPK traffic forecast for 2015–2035 CAGR of 4.4%.

4.2 Offset Demand Outlook in All Phases, 2021–2035

Pre-COVID-19 ICAO forecasts point to a continuous increase in demand for CORSIA carbon credits: aggregate demand from 2021 to 2035 is estimated at 2.5 billion metric tons of CO_2e (tCO_2e). The post-COVID-19 modeling scenarios (slow recovery subdued growth; fast recovery trend growth) introduced in this report suggest that offset demand over this time period could be from 1 billion to 2 billion tCO_2e (Figure 8).[37] Both pre-COVID-19 and post-COVID-19 modeling point to a significant increase in demand for carbon offsets from 2027 onward, as the CORSIA scheme becomes mandatory across all states that are not exempt.

---

[37] From 2021 to 2035, under the "slow recovery subdued growth" scenario, total offset demand is estimated at 1,045 million tCO_2e whereas under the "fast recovery trend growth" scenario total offset demand is estimated at 2,069 million tCO_2e. For comparison, the pre-COVID-19 ICAO forecasts of offset demand for this time period is estimated at 2,515 million tCO_2e.

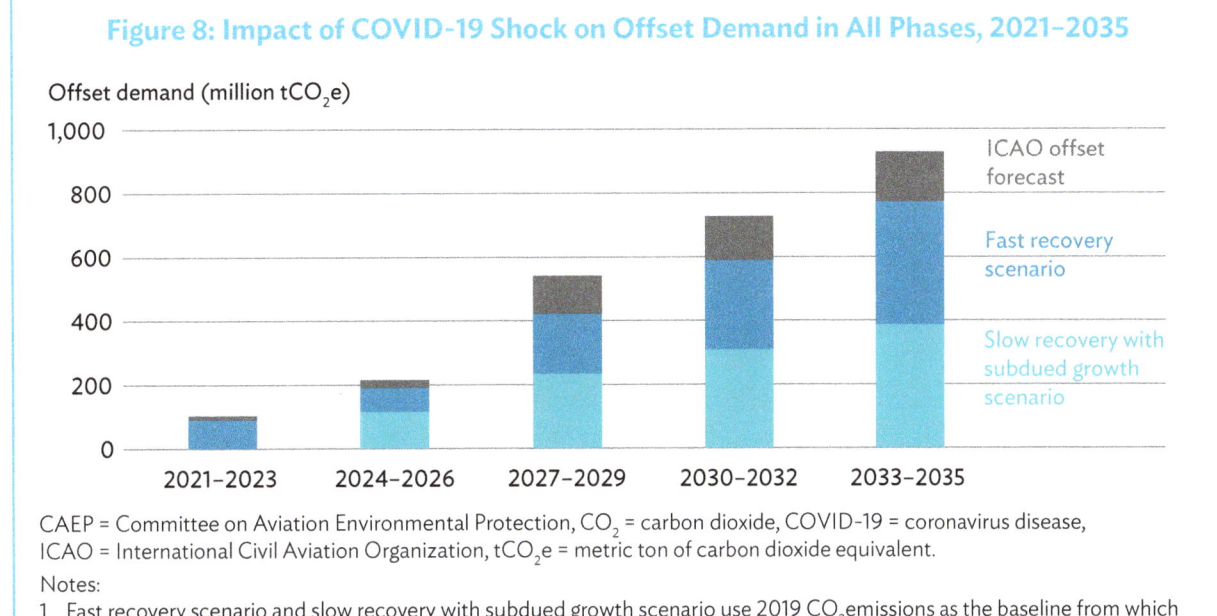

Figure 8: Impact of COVID-19 Shock on Offset Demand in All Phases, 2021–2035

CAEP = Committee on Aviation Environmental Protection, CO_2 = carbon dioxide, COVID-19 = coronavirus disease, ICAO = International Civil Aviation Organization, tCO_2e = metric ton of carbon dioxide equivalent.

Notes:
1. Fast recovery scenario and slow recovery with subdued growth scenario use 2019 CO_2 emissions as the baseline from which to calculate offset responsibility; coverage goes from 57% in the beginning to 90% from 2027.
2. CO_2 emissions are estimated in proportion to international passenger air transport traffic performed by carriers registered within each region.
3. ICAO offset forecast was done prior to COVID-19 shock.

Source: Asian Development Bank using ICAO data on CO_2 offset forecast, CAEP 11 forecast, and annual reports.

To date, the Clean Development Mechanism (CDM) is the main mechanism under the United Nations Framework Convention on Climate Change (UNFCCC) framework through which developing countries can create tradable emission credits. It is therefore relevant to compare projected CORSIA demand to the historical generation of offsets under the CDM, which amounts to about 2 billion tCO_2e in certified emission reductions (CERs). So, even after taking into account COVID-19 impacts, demand for carbon offsets from international aviation between 2021 and 2035 is likely to be of the same order of magnitude of all the CERs issued up to April 2020, since the first CER issuance in 2007.

Scheme Coverage Significantly Impacts Offset Demand

Several large aviation states, including India, the People's Republic of China, and the Russian Federation, have filed reservations to ICAO's global aspiration goals and have rejected CORSIA design elements in part or in full. If these states do not join CORSIA, it will significantly reduce CORSIA demand for offsets. In 2018, the international air traffic performed by airlines registered in these states amounted to about 16.6% of the total. Further, even if exempt states, representing half of exempt traffic, elect to voluntarily participate in the scheme, the remaining 5% of exempt international traffic of airlines registered in exempt states will not be covered. On aggregate, this means that 21.6% of international activity would not be covered by the scheme. Since exemptions would extend to all flights performed to and from the exempt states and not only to the airlines registered there, the relative share of international CO_2 emissions not covered by the scheme would be about 30%–40%, thus, only about 60%–70% of international CO_2 emissions would be covered under CORSIA.

However, there is room for cautious optimism regarding future prospects for broader coverage under CORSIA. Voluntary participation in CORSIA has been impressive from the outset. As of 3 April 2020, states representing 76.64% of international aviation activity had joined the scheme.[38] Further, ICAO has approved carbon crediting mechanisms, such as the CDM and the China GHG Voluntary Emission Reduction Program, that would allow countries like India and the People's Republic of China to source offsets from domestic carbon reduction projects if they participate voluntarily in the pilot phase. The list of eligible carbon-crediting mechanisms could further expand in the future. The participation of national carbon-crediting mechanisms in CORSIA may reduce resistance to the scheme.

Offset Demand Could Be Boosted by Voluntary Action

Irrespective of compliance requirements under CORSIA, airlines or their passengers may voluntarily take on greater climate action. This may in turn lead to the introduction of more stringent offsetting requirements following CORSIA's periodic reviews.[39] The International Airlines Group (IAG, the parent company of Aer Lingus, British Airways, Iberia, Level, and Vueling) announced in October of 2019 its commitment to achieving net zero carbon emission by 2050.[40] In February 2020, Delta Air Lines announced its commitment to $1 billion in funding over 10 years for investments in becoming fully carbon neutral.[41] If Delta's commitment was to be scaled up at the industry level, demand for offsets from international aviation over the 2021–2035 time period could exceed 10 billion tCO_2e, even after taking into account robust implementation of mitigation actions within the aviation sector.

Improvements in Aircraft Design and Sustainable Aviation Fuels Can Reduce Demand for Offsets

Improvements in both the airframes of aircraft and in engine technology are expected to be evolutionary up to about 2035, with traditional tube-and-wing configuration and turbofan engines powered by jet fuel. Assuming continued fleet renewal practices and operational advances, such evolutionary innovations in aircraft design can help to maintain fuel efficiency improvements broadly consistent with historical trends. Revolutionary new aircraft configurations and propulsion systems will not likely be ready for entry into service before 2035.[42] Until then, technology improvements are unlikely to exceed historical rates of improvement. Therefore, demand for carbon offsets will not be materially impacted by revolutionary technologies during the CORSIA program period.

The only technological development that could potentially deliver greater reductions in CO_2 emissions prior to 2035 could come from the commercialization of sustainable aviation fuels (SAF). However, the uptake of SAFs has been much slower than expected. Given the significant gap in commercializing existing SAF pathways (Box 2), the analysis in this report does not directly consider the impact of SAF on overall global offset demand during the 2021–2035 time period.

---

[38] ICAO. 2020. *Document: CORSIA States for Chapter 3 State Pairs*. July. https://www.icao.int/environmental-protection/CORSIA/Pages/state-pairs.aspx.
[39] The ICAO Council is scheduled to start its first review in 2022, with subsequent reviews taking place every 3 years.
[40] International Airline Group (IAG). 2019. IAG Backs Net Zero Emissions by 2050. 10 October. https://www.iairgroup.com/en/newsroom/press-releases/newsroom-listing/2019/net-zero-emissions.
[41] The 10-year funding period started on 1 March 2020. Delta Air Lines. 2020. Delta Commits $1 Billion to Become First Carbon Neutral Airline Globally. 14 February. https://news.delta.com/delta-commits-1-billion-become-first-carbon-neutral-airline-globally.
[42] IATA. Aircraft Technology Roadmap to 2050. Geneva. https://www.iata.org/contentassets/8d19e716636a47c184e7221c77563c93/technology20roadmap20to20205020no20foreword.pdf.

> **Box 2: Long-Term Potential of Sustainable Aviation Fuels**
>
> As of May 2020, about 250,000 commercial flights have been operated using a blend of conventional jet fuel and sustainable aviation fuels (SAF).[a] Commercial production of SAF has increased from 0.29 million liters per year (2013–2015) to 6.45 million liters per year (2016–2018).[b] Despite this impressive growth, SAF represented less than 0.002% of total fuel used by commercial aviation in the 2016–2018 period.
>
> McKinsey estimates that SAF production costs about $3,000 per metric ton, which is more than 10 times the current jet fuel price ($239 per metric ton).[c] Even if jet fuel prices recover to pre-coronavirus disease levels of about $75 per barrel or about $600 per metric ton, SAF production costs are expected to be three to five times the cost of conventional jet fuel. SAF is not expected to become price competitive with conventional jet fuel before 2035.
>
> Despite the difficulties with commercial scalability of SAF, production volumes may continue to rise. Isolated opportunities may emerge where there is a combination of government support, abundant feedstock, and cheap inputs for energy conversion. While these developments could make a substantial difference to some individual airlines' offset requirements, it is highly uncertain whether they will have a material impact on fuel consumption across the industry by 2035.
>
> [a] Air Transport Action Group. Aviation Benefits Beyond Borders. Sustainable Aviation Fuel. https://aviationbenefits.org/environmental-efficiency/climate-action/sustainable-aviation-fuel.
> [b] International Civil Aviation Organization (ICAO). 2019. Destination Green: The Next Chapter. *ICAO Environmental Report 2019: Aviation and Environment*. Chapter 1. https://www.icao.int/environmental-protection/Pages/envrep2019.aspx.
> [c] A. Dichter et al. 2020. How Airlines Can Chart a Path to Zero-Carbon Flying. *McKinsey & Company*. 13 May. https://www.mckinsey.com/industries/travel-logistics-and-transport-infrastructure/our-insights/how-airlines-can-chart-a-path-to-zero-carbon-flying.
>
> Source: Asian Development Bank.

4.3 Offset Demand Outlook in the Pilot Phase, 2021–2023

The following three factors significantly influence the near-term outlook for offset demand during the CORSIA pilot phase:

(i) pace of aviation industry recovery from COVID-19,
(ii) share of international aviation activity covered by CORSIA, and
(iii) revisions to the baseline.

In the pilot phase, demand for carbon offsets from international aviation will likely be below the reference figures disseminated by ICAO prior to the COVID-19 shock (104 million tCO_2e).[43] As per the scenarios presented in Section 4.1, pilot phase demand could range from 0 to 92 million tCO_2e, depending on the pace of the industry's recovery.

Although 83 states, representing 76.64% of international aviation activity (footnote 38), had expressed their intention to voluntarily participate in CORSIA from its outset as of April 2020, the share of airline activity covered represents less than 57% of CO_2 emissions from international air transport.[44]

---

[43] ICAO. 2019. CORSIA Frequently Asked Questions. 31 October. https://www.icao.int/environmental-protection/CORSIA/Documents/CORSIA_FAQs_October%202019_final.pdf.
[44] This estimate is generated based on applying the exemption criteria to the Organisation for Economic Co-operation and Development (OECD) air transport CO_2 emission estimates for international aviation in 2018.

The post-COVID-19 adjustment of the base year for evaluating progress toward the zero net growth target also has important implications. The same two post-COVID-19 recovery scenarios introduced in the previous section have been used to estimate the impact on offset demand in the pilot phase (Figure 9).[45]

- Under the slow recovery and subdued growth scenario, aviation CO_2 emissions in 2021 are 20% lower than 2019. CO_2 emissions return to 2019 levels in 2022 and exceed 2019 levels in 2023 by about 8%. However, since the sum of the annual CO_2 emissions growth relative to the 2019 is negative for the 3-year pilot phase period, there is no demand for carbon offsets.

- Under the fast recovery and trend growth scenario, international aviation rebounds to trend growth in 2021 that is consistent with the ICAO 20-year forecast for 2015–2035. Offset demand during the pilot phase is estimated at about 92 million tCO_2e, or about 12 million metric tons below the pre-COVID-19 forecast of ICAO. If the COVID-19 epidemiological situation does not improve immediately, the likelihood of this scenario materializing reduces significantly and the recovery will be delayed. Nevertheless, this scenario is included in the analysis as it serves as a relevant reference point.

In terms of timing, airlines are allowed to manage their offset liabilities in whatever way they deem most appropriate. However, by 31 January 2025, aircraft operators are required to submit reports confirming that they have cancelled sufficient emission units to be in compliance under the pilot phase (2021–2023). Some airlines may choose to proactively manage their offset liabilities by taking advantage of current historically low carbon offset prices. Others may choose to purchase offsets on a rolling basis, incorporating offset management into the normal flow of operating expenses. The balance between such strategies will impact the timing of demand.

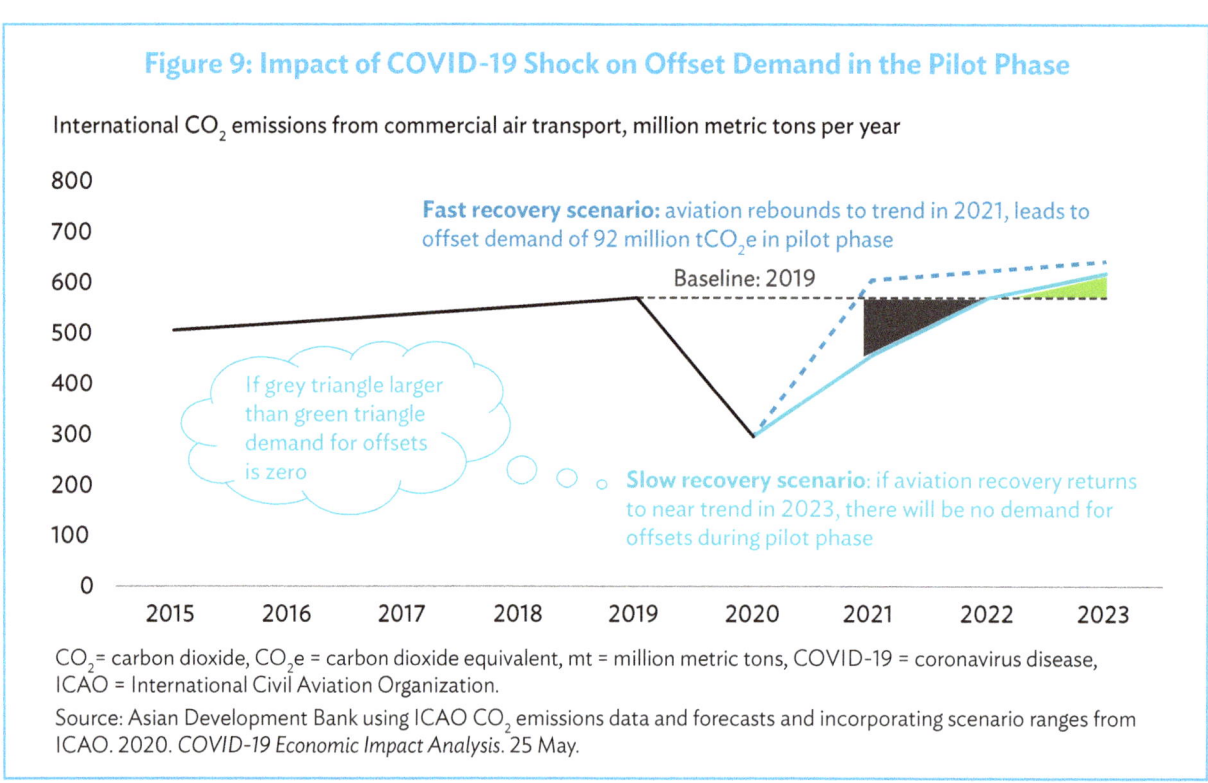

Figure 9: Impact of COVID-19 Shock on Offset Demand in the Pilot Phase

CO_2 = carbon dioxide, CO_2e = carbon dioxide equivalent, mt = million metric tons, COVID-19 = coronavirus disease, ICAO = International Civil Aviation Organization.
Source: Asian Development Bank using ICAO CO_2 emissions data and forecasts and incorporating scenario ranges from ICAO. 2020. *COVID-19 Economic Impact Analysis*. 25 May.

---

[45] The aggregate growth profile depicted in each of the scenarios assumes an equivalent growth profile for routes covered by CORSIA and those exempt from the scheme.

4.4 Offset Demand in Asia and the Pacific

In 2018, airlines registered in ADB developing member countries (DMCs) represented about 27% of total international traffic. By 3 April 2020, 42% of international traffic performed by airlines registered in DMCs was already volunteered by governments to participate in the pilot phase of CORSIA. By 2027, about 95% of the international activity performed by DMC airlines will be either under mandatory coverage or participating in the scheme voluntarily (Figure 10). The demand for carbon offsets from DMC airlines will be substantial.

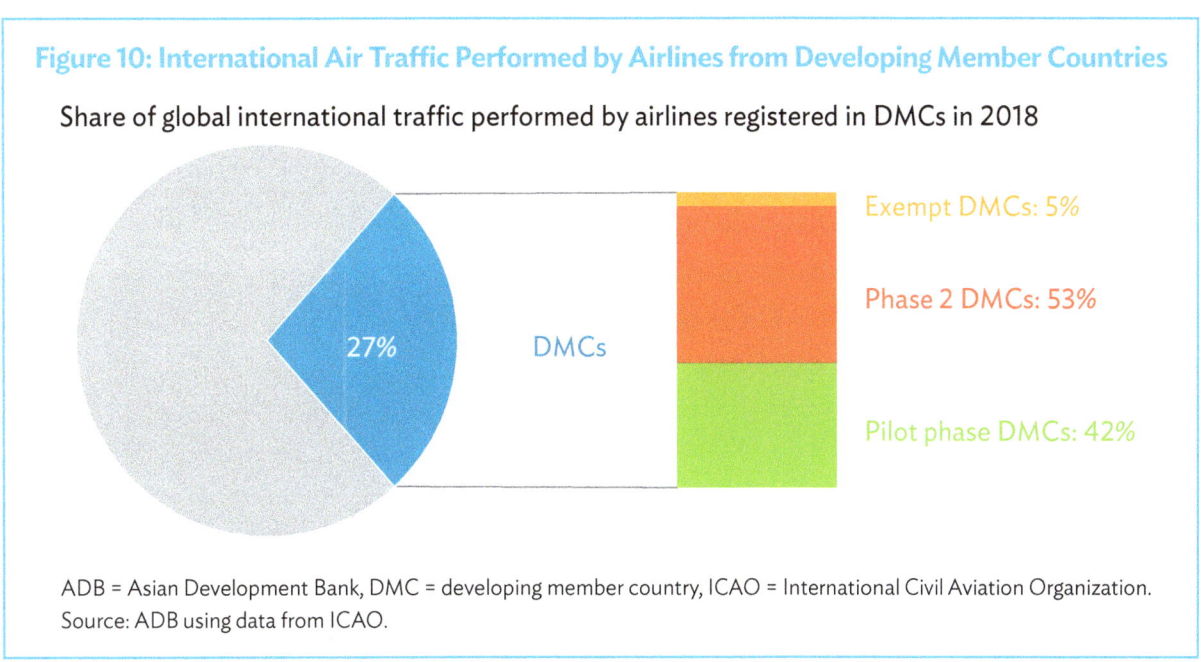

Figure 10: International Air Traffic Performed by Airlines from Developing Member Countries

Share of global international traffic performed by airlines registered in DMCs in 2018

- Exempt DMCs: 5%
- Phase 2 DMCs: 53%
- Pilot phase DMCs: 42%

ADB = Asian Development Bank, DMC = developing member country, ICAO = International Civil Aviation Organization.
Source: ADB using data from ICAO.

Airlines in Asia and the Pacific are expected to continue to be among the fastest-growing and may become the largest buyers of CORSIA offsets over the duration of the program (2021–2035). The forecast presented in Figure 11 applies the relative historic (2013–2018) growth dynamic to the ICAO 20-year (2015–2035) global forecast with an additional adjustment in line with the slow recovery and subdued growth scenario. It provides a relevant reference point for the future offset demand of airlines registered across different regions. However, this forecast does not consider potential participation gaps or the application of exemptions, which could lead to lower offset demand from regions with less comprehensive CORSIA route coverage.

The relative growth rates across regions over the 2021–2035 period may differ compared to the historical reference point. Nevertheless, on aggregate, airlines in Asia are expected to continue to be among the fastest-growing globally during this time period. Airlines in Asia and Africa may experience relatively higher growth rates, as regional initiatives targeting aviation market liberalization gain momentum. Beyond sector drivers, aviation growth in emerging markets is expected to continue to be driven by favorable demographic trends and rising per capita income. Regions that may experience lower relative growth compared to historical trends include the Middle East and Europe.[46] Considering these factors, Figure 11 likely understates the relative future share of carbon offset demand of airlines in Asia.

---

[46] The expansion of Middle Eastern carriers was expected to decelerate even prior to COVID-19. Similarly, with the boost to aviation growth rates that resulted from moving to a single aviation market fading, European airlines were also expected to experience a deceleration of growth.

A significant portion of the growth of European carriers depicted in Figure 11 corresponds to international flights within the European Economic Area. These flights are considered international by ICAO, but are currently within the scope of the European Union Emission Trading Scheme.[47] The relative share of CORSIA credits demanded by airlines in Europe may be lower than depicted in the chart, if airline compliance for those emissions is limited to surrendering of European Union Allowances and European Union Aviation Allowances for intra-European Economic Area flights, as is currently the case. If so, the relative share of CORSIA compliant offsets that would be demanded by airlines in Asia is likely to be larger than depicted in Figure 11.

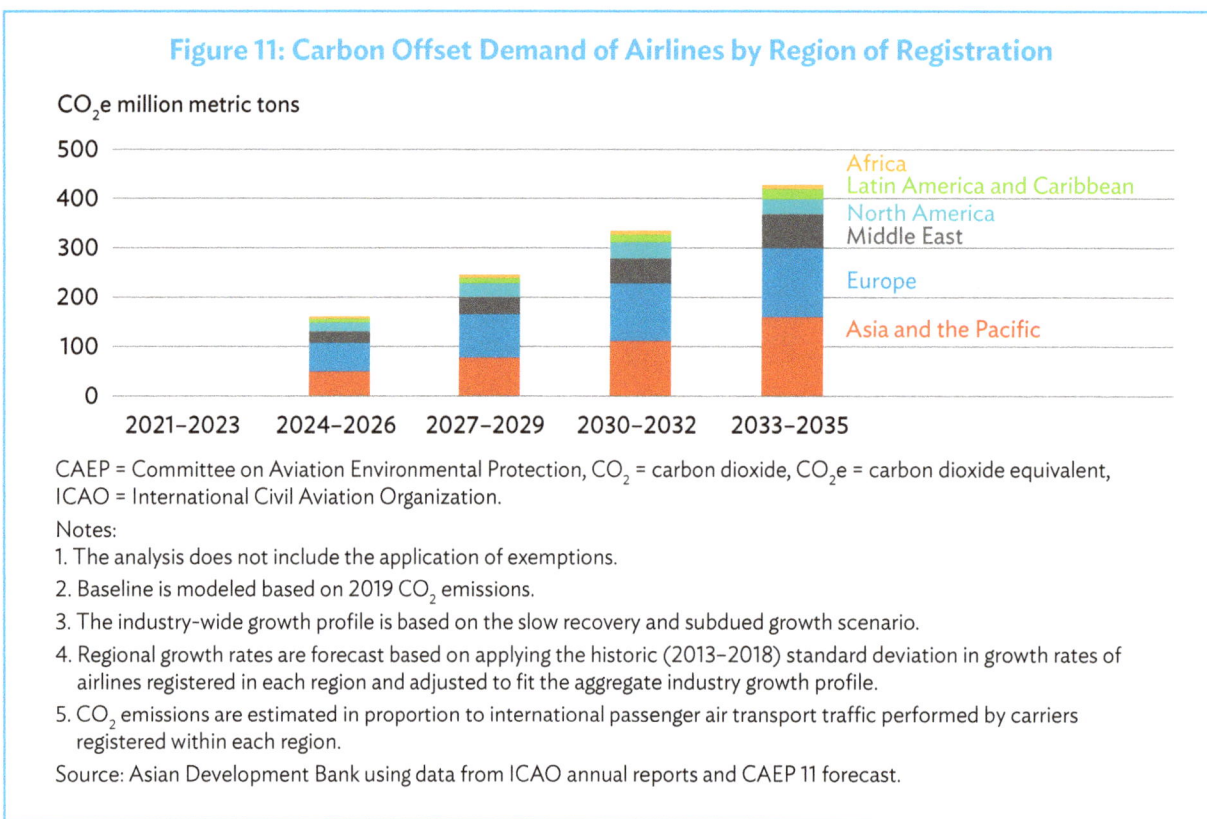

Figure 11: Carbon Offset Demand of Airlines by Region of Registration

CAEP = Committee on Aviation Environmental Protection, CO_2 = carbon dioxide, CO_2e = carbon dioxide equivalent, ICAO = International Civil Aviation Organization.

Notes:
1. The analysis does not include the application of exemptions.
2. Baseline is modeled based on 2019 CO_2 emissions.
3. The industry-wide growth profile is based on the slow recovery and subdued growth scenario.
4. Regional growth rates are forecast based on applying the historic (2013–2018) standard deviation in growth rates of airlines registered in each region and adjusted to fit the aggregate industry growth profile.
5. CO_2 emissions are estimated in proportion to international passenger air transport traffic performed by carriers registered within each region.

Source: Asian Development Bank using data from ICAO annual reports and CAEP 11 forecast.

Some states, including Brazil and the US, have filed reservations to specific elements of ICAO resolutions related to criteria for supplying offsets. This suggests that some states may treat the ICAO-approved offset sources as a menu to choose from, allowing only some of the mechanisms approved by ICAO to be used by airlines for compliance. Therefore, suppliers of CORSIA-eligible offsets in Asia may face constraints in supplying some airlines, especially outside the region. Nevertheless, carbon credit suppliers in Asia are unlikely to be left stranded, as there will still be plenty of demand for offsets specifically from DMC airlines.

Table 2 presents potential offset demand under the CORSIA pilot phase (2021–2023) and first phase (2024-2026) for a selection of DMCs. The scenarios presented in the columns of the table illustrate a range of potential offset demand. For each country, carbon offset demand is estimated by applying the growth curves resulting from the two scenarios presented here (specifically the slow recovery and subdued growth scenario, and the fast recovery and trend growth scenario) to the 2018 international CO_2 emissions from airlines registered in the respective DMCs.[48]

---

[47] In 2019, 68.14 million tCO_2e of CO_2 was emitted on domestic and international flights within the European Economic Area. European Commission. 2020. Emissions Trading: Greenhouse Gas Emission Reduced by 8.7% in 2019. 4 May. https://ec.europa.eu/clima/news/emissions-trading-greenhouse-gas-emissions-reduced-87-2019_en.

[48] The international CO_2 emissions for 2018 were estimated using OECD modeling as the primary input for the data analysis. OECD Stat. Air Transport CO_2 Emissions. https://stats.oecd.org/Index.aspx?DataSetCode=AIRTRANS_CO2 (accessed 24 May 2020).

Table 2: Offset Demand for Select Developing Member Countries, 2021–2026

Country	Pilot phase, mt CO_2e			First phase, mt CO_2e		
	100% coverage	57% coverage	Slow recovery, subdued	100% coverage	57% coverage	Slow recovery, subdued
China, People's Republic of	14.4	8.2	0.0	28.8	16.4	8.8
Korea, Republic of	9.5	5.4	0.0	18.9	10.8	5.8
Singapore	7.0	4.0	0.0	14.0	8.0	4.3
Thailand	4.7	2.7	0.0	9.3	5.3	2.8
India	3.6	2.1	0.0	7.2	4.1	2.2
Malaysia	3.4	1.9	0.0	6.7	3.8	2.0
Philippines	2.0	1.2	0.0	4.0	2.3	1.2
Indonesia	1.7	1.0	0.0	3.4	1.9	1.0
Viet Nam	1.3	0.7	0.0	2.6	1.5	0.8
Sri Lanka	0.7	0.4	0.0	1.3	0.8	0.4
Pakistan	0.7	0.4	0.0	1.3	0.8	0.4
Azerbaijan	0.6	0.3	0.0	1.1	0.6	0.3
Bangladesh	0.4	0.2	0.0	0.8	0.5	0.3
Kazakhstan	0.4	0.2	0.0	0.7	0.4	0.2
Uzbekistan	0.3	0.2	0.0	0.6	0.4	0.2
Fiji	0.3	0.1	0.0	0.5	0.3	0.2
Brunei Darussalam	0.2	0.1	0.0	0.4	0.2	0.1
Cambodia	0.1	0.1	0.0	0.3	0.2	0.1
Turkmenistan	0.1	0.1	0.0	0.2	0.1	0.1
Papua New Guinea	0.1	0.0	0.0	0.2	0.1	0.0
Nepal	0.1	0.0	0.0	0.2	0.1	0.0
Tajikistan	0.1	0.0	0.0	0.1	0.1	0.0
Georgia	0.1	0.0	0.0	0.1	0.1	0.0
Afghanistan	0.1	0.0	0.0	0.1	0.1	0.0
Mongolia	0.1	0.0	0.0	0.1	0.1	0.0
Myanmar	0.0	0.0	0.0	0.1	0.1	0.0

CORSIA = Carbon Offsetting and Reduction Scheme for International Aviation, DMC = developing member country, mt CO_2e = million metric tons of carbon dioxide equivalent, OECD = Organisation for Economic Co-operation and Development.

Notes:
1. Countries are listed in descending order (largest to smallest) by volume of offset demanded.
2. The list includes graduated DMCs.
3. Several of the DMCs listed in the table above have not expressed their intention to voluntarily participate in the pilot and first phases of the CORSIA scheme.
4. Those not participating in the scheme will have an offset demand equal to zero.

Source: Asian Development Bank using data from OECD.

The scenarios labeled 100% coverage and 57% coverage are estimates of offset demand under the fast recovery and trend growth scenario for airlines registered in the respective DMCs. Under 100% coverage, 100% of the country's international aviation CO_2 emissions are assumed to be covered by the CORSIA scheme. Under the 57% coverage, 57% (equivalent to the current global coverage) of the country's international aviation CO_2 emissions is assumed to be covered by the CORSIA scheme. Offset demand is estimated against the 2019 baseline.

The slow recovery and subdued growth scenario is modeled applying the average industry growth rate in CO_2 emissions from this scenario to the 2018 international CO_2 emission from airlines registered in the respective DMCs. The scheme coverage for individual countries in this scenario is assumed to be 57% (equivalent to the current global coverage). Again, offset demand is estimated against the 2019 baseline.

Box 3: Offsetting Airline Carbon Dioxide Emissions in the Republic of Korea

The Republic of Korea (ROK) plays an important role in the global air transport network. Prior to the coronavirus shock, scheduled air transport activity (measured in revenue ton kilometers) performed by airlines registered in the ROK was the sixth-largest in the world, trailing German airlines and ahead of the Russian Federation airlines. In Asia and the Pacific, only airlines registered in the People's Republic of China performed more air transport activity. In 2018, international air services accounted for over 95% of scheduled air transport activity of airlines registered in the ROK.[a] In terms of emissions, over 90% of carbon dioxide (CO_2) emissions of airlines from the ROK were emitted on international air services, with the remaining share attributed to domestic operations.[b]

The domestic air transport industry is one of the sectors that was included in the National Emission Trading Scheme of the ROK (KETS) since 2015. Internationally, the ROK has already committed to participate voluntarily in the Carbon Offsetting and Reduction Scheme for International Aviation (CORSIA) from its outset. Although there is high uncertainty in the pace of the recovery of demand for air transport, Korean Air anticipates that airlines registered in the ROK will purchase offsets worth about $850 million from 2021 to 2035.[c] Airlines registered in the ROK are expected to become one of the major buyers of carbon offsets for CORSIA compliance. While this is an opportunity for international carbon trading, this potential can only be fully realized if rules for carbon trading are predictable and coherent with the broader climate policy framework.

The ROK has the potential to provide a model for sound climate policy development. The opportunity would materialize if it succeeds in putting in place consistent policies and transparent accounting rules that avoid double counting of mitigation efforts with respect to its national climate mitigation target, international cooperation under the Paris Agreement, and the use of CORSIA units. As part of its nationally determined contribution, the ROK has indicated that it will partly use carbon credits from international market mechanisms to achieve its 2030 mitigation target.[d] Further, within phase III (2021–2025) of the KETS, the Government of the ROK intends to allow the use of international credits and has developed a plan for the establishment of an international cooperation system. While details of the plan are still under deliberation, it represents a significant policy opportunity. If in combination with these efforts, the ROK elaborates on how CORSIA compliant units will be accounted for as part of this framework, it could offer a model for other countries to follow for ensuring avoidance of double counting of emission reductions, while offering greater policy predictability.

[a] International Civil Aviation Organization. 2019. Annual Report of the Council. Presentation of 2018 Air Transport Statistical Results, Table 5.
[b] The international CO_2 emissions for 2018 were estimated using Organisation for Economic Co-operation and Development (OECD) modeling as the primary input for the data analysis. OECD Stat. Air Transport CO_2 Emissions. https://stats.oecd.org/Index.aspx?DataSetCode=AIRTRANS_CO2 (accessed 24 May 2020).
[c] Interviews with Korean Air in 2020.
[d] United Nations Framework Convention on Climate Change. 2015. Submission of the Republic of Korea, Intended Nationally Determined Contribution. 30 June.

Source: Asian Development Bank.

4.5 Other Potential Sources of Offset Demand from Aviation

Globally, in 2015, domestic aviation made up 35% of global commercial air transport emissions (Figure 12). In Asia, several large domestic aviation markets exist and have been among the world's fastest-growing. Asia's share of domestic passengers is second only to that of North America. In 2019, 7 out of 10 passengers in Asia boarding an aircraft were doing so to take a domestic flight (footnote 31).

In the aviation industry, it is common practice to transpose internationally agreed standards and recommended practices to domestic aviation. A harmonized approach across domestic and international air services can help avoid market distortions, reduce regulatory burden, and avoid costly domestic measures. Applying solutions developed through CORSIA as a way to align domestic aviation CO_2 emissions with nationally determined contribution (NDC) targets and Paris Agreement temperature goals, could potentially create another source of demand for carbon offsets. For example, airlines could be allowed to meet their relevant national climate targets for domestic aviation through the purchase of CORSIA-eligible carbon offsets.

This is a major opportunity for policy development, as many DMCs have not yet identified policies within their NDCs for addressing CO_2 emissions from domestic aviation. Alignment of domestic targets and approaches to meeting them could also be important to efforts to limit market distortions between domestic and international travel markets.

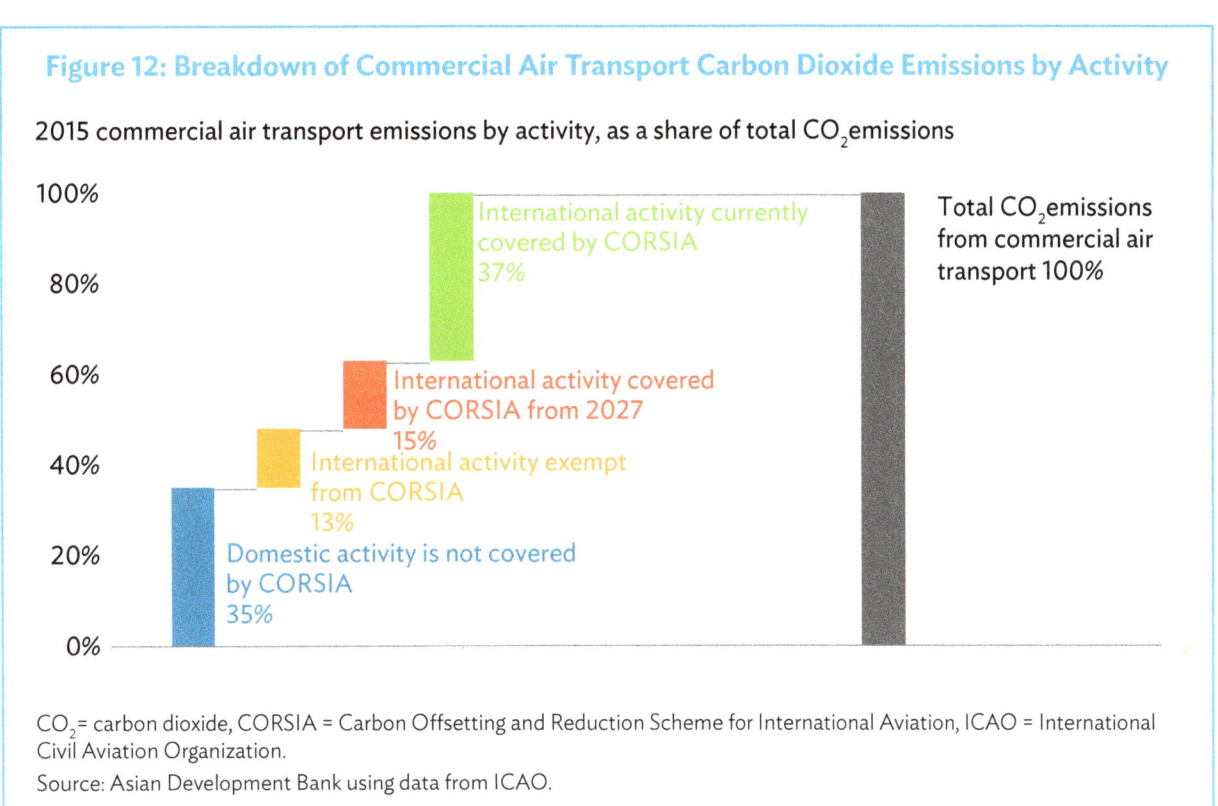

Figure 12: Breakdown of Commercial Air Transport Carbon Dioxide Emissions by Activity

CO_2 = carbon dioxide, CORSIA = Carbon Offsetting and Reduction Scheme for International Aviation, ICAO = International Civil Aviation Organization.
Source: Asian Development Bank using data from ICAO.

5 Challenges and Opportunities for Supplying Offsets from Asia

This section focuses on some of the key challenges specific to supplying offsets to CORSIA and opportunities for climate policy makers and ADB DMCs to overcome them.

5.1 Climate Policy Makers in Developing Member Countries

Pilot Phase, 2021–2023

Challenge 1: Double counting, especially double claiming of carbon credits

Given the ongoing negotiations on accounting rules under the Paris Agreement, airlines are likely to be cautious about sourcing offsets from jurisdictions and activities that may fall under the Paris Agreement. In particular, they will likely attempt to avoid purchasing offsets generated in countries where there is a perceived risk of the offsets also being counted against the nationally determined contribution (NDC), since it is not yet clear if, and to what extent, certified emission reductions (CERs) from pre-2020 projects will be allowed for use against NDCs. In the absence of internationally agreed accounting rules, there may also be a risk of double claiming if an intermediary in a third-party country is involved. Through inventive accounting, a third party may successfully claim emission reductions while reselling carbon credits to airlines. Lack of harmonized accounting rules and an absence of focus on avoiding double counting could lead to erode environmental credibility.

Opportunity. For the first pilot phase, DMC policy makers can better position their carbon offset suppliers for CORSIA by filling the gap in the international rules and proactively putting in place clear policies on how to prevent double counting between national mitigation action, international cooperation and CORSIA related credits. In addition, policy makers can support efforts that allow airlines to directly purchase emission reductions from national projects. For example, enacting a clear and non-discriminatory tax policy across all offset purchasers, such as through a uniform tax exemption for carbon credits, can reduce anxiety for airline purchases of emission reductions from owners of national projects.

All Phases, 2021–2035

Challenge 2: Disjointed policies on domestic mitigation and international cooperation

The rules for international cooperation under the Paris Agreement are still under negotiation, which makes it difficult to develop coherent policies and, in particular, a complete set of technical regulations and guidelines.

There is a risk that in the absence of strategic foresight, policy development may become disjointed or conflicted across approaches for domestic mitigation actions, international crediting mechanisms, and the generation of CORSIA carbon offsets. A disjointed policy framework could hinder climate action and will make it more difficult to deliver CORSIA-compliant credits at a scale that is likely to be required in future demand scenarios.

Opportunity. DMC policy makers can focus on ensuring policy coherence as it relates to their NDC, international cooperation under the Paris Agreement, and supply of carbon offsets to CORSIA. This may entail identifying how to make policy-level mechanisms simultaneously deliver contributions to achieving NDC targets and internationally transferred mitigation outcomes that can be used for CORSIA compliance. Similarly, clarifying under what conditions mitigation actions fall within one category and not the other (i.e., are expected to contribute to achieving the national NDC or to generate exportable offsets) can offer greater policy clarity.

Challenge 3: Lack of access by developing member countries to desired mechanisms for generating CORSIA-eligible offsets

Some DMCs may be inhibited in accessing mechanisms approved under CORSIA for generating offsets. Access to mechanisms may be constrained because of a mismatch between the local circumstances of project developers and design features of the approved mechanisms. Other barriers to DMCs accessing mechanisms include geographical limitations of approved mechanisms and the incidence of higher transaction costs for DMCs.

Opportunity. DMC policy makers can support the adoption of policies that make it easier to deploy approved mechanisms under CORSIA in DMCs. For example, DMC policy makers could recognize (through legal and administrative measures) some of the CORSIA-approved offset mechanisms and take steps that make it easier for relevant service providers (such as verification and validation agencies accredited by the respective mechanisms) to operate locally.

5.2 Carbon Offset Suppliers from Developing Member Countries

Pilot Phase, 2021–2023

Challenge 4: Little or no demand for offset credits due to coronavirus diseases shock.

There is a possibility that there will be little or no demand for carbon offsets in the pilot phase. This could result in an absence of information flow between offset buyers and sellers, which could have adverse long-term consequences on market dynamics (after the pilot phase). If the lack of market functioning in the pilot phase is not complemented by information exchanges, it will be more difficult to reveal future premium qualities within eligible offset mechanisms. A lack of exchange of information may also lead to missed opportunities for creating voluntary offsetting partnerships between offset suppliers, airlines, passengers, and shippers.

Opportunity. DMC carbon offset suppliers could support two-way information exchange initiatives between offset suppliers and airlines that are geared toward voluntary offsetting. Voluntary offsetting arrangements have the potential to create demand for carbon credits by tapping climate conscious consumers interested in offsetting their travel and shipping services. Voluntary offsetting could also explore using information exchanges to identify what offset qualities airlines value, and to improve their understanding of the demand from specific airlines and the anticipated timing of future offset purchases by airlines. Arrangements developed in the context of voluntary offsetting could be transitioned to focus on CORSIA compliance when offset demand picks-up in future phases.

All Phases, 2021–2035

Challenge 5: A lack of appetite of airlines to purchase offsets from developing countries

Some individual airlines and groups of airlines may have an appetite to source offset credits from primary markets.[49] This appetite may even exist in the pilot phase, if there is a rapid recovery after the coronavirus disease (COVID-19) shock. However, individual offset projects face project-specific risks that can lead to an under-delivery of offset credits.[50] Under-delivery of contracted offsets can impose additional costs to buyers if the buyer is forced to source higher-priced offsets from the spot market (secondary market) or incur penalties due to noncompliance.[51]

Furthermore, country specific risk should be considered. This may include host country approval for the transfer of credits abroad or even as a result of host country retroactive claims on previously approved carbon credit transfers. For example, in future periods of CORSIA, the transfer of carbon credits to a CORSIA buyer may require an approval by the host country where the activity generates emission reductions. In instances when the emission reductions are generated from within the scope of the NDC, the host country will likely need to make a corresponding adjustment to its NDC or emissions balance. There could be risks related to both receiving such an approval and of having approvals retracted in light of challenges for the host country to achieve the NDC.

The combination of project-specific risks and higher countrywide risk factors can create an unbearably high-risk perception for implementing projects in developing countries.[52] Therefore, the risk profiles of individual projects may be unacceptable to offset buyers.

Opportunity. Offset suppliers can address the appetites of purchasing airlines by participating in carbon fund vehicles. In addition to managing underperformance risk through project pooling and other risk management techniques, tailored carbon funds have the potential to incorporate design features most appealing to airlines, while securing future revenue streams for offset suppliers in DMCs. Sourcing offsets through carbon funds in host countries that prohibit double claiming of CORSIA emission reductions may also mitigate the risk of double claiming.

---

[49] Secondary markets already exist for the approved offset types and generally take the form of over-the-counter transactions, although in some instances some offset credits are traded on exchanges.
[50] World Bank. 2007. *Uzbekistan Carbon Finance for New Project: A Primer.* 14 January. http://documents.worldbank.org/curated/en/917621468338451727/pdf/707460ESW0P10000brief0final0011807.pdf.
[51] In some instances, buyers can manage these risks through contract provisions that transfer the higher costs incurred due to under-delivery to offset suppliers. However, such contracts still carry counterparty risk and in practice may be unrealistic to enforce.
[52] OECD. 2020. Prevailing Country Risk Classification. https://www.oecd.org/trade/topics/export-credits/arrangement-and-sector-understandings/financing-terms-and-conditions/country-risk-classification/.

APPENDIX 1
Carbon Offsetting and Reduction Scheme for International Aviation Emissions Unit Eligibility Criteria

Program design elements. At the program level, the International Civil Aviation Organization (ICAO) should ensure that eligible offset credit programs meet the following design elements:[1]

(i) ***Clear methodologies and protocols, and their development process.*** Programs should have qualification and quantification methodologies and protocols in place and available for use as well as a process for developing further methodologies and protocols. The existing methodologies and protocols as well as the process for developing further methodologies and protocols should be publicly disclosed.

(ii) ***Scope considerations.*** Programs should define and publicly disclose the level at which activities are allowed under the program (e.g., project-based, program of activities, etc.) as well as the eligibility criteria for each type of offset activity (e.g., which sectors, project types, or geographic locations are covered).

(iii) ***Offset credit issuance and retirement procedures.*** Programs should have in place procedures for how offset credits are: (a) issued, (b) retired or cancelled, (c) subject to any discounting, and (d) the length of the crediting period and whether that period is renewable. These procedures should be publicly disclosed.

(iv) ***Identification and tracking.*** Programs should have in place procedures that ensure that: (a) units are tracked; (b) units are individually identified through serial numbers, (c) registry is secure (i.e., robust security provisions are in place); and (d) units have clearly identified owners or holders (e.g., identification requirements of a registry). The program should also stipulate (a) to which, if any, other registries it is linked; and, (b) whether and which international data exchange standards the registry conforms with. All of the above should be publicly disclosed information.

(v) ***Legal nature and transfer of units.*** The program should define and ensure the underlying attributes and property aspects of a unit, and publicly disclose the process by which it does so.

(vi) ***Validation and verification procedures.*** Programs should have in place validation and verification standards and procedures, as well as requirements and procedures for the accreditation of validators and verifiers. All of the above mentioned standards, procedures, and requirements should be publicly disclosed.

(vii) ***Program governance.*** Programs should publicly disclose who is responsible for administration of the program and how decisions are made.

(viii) ***Transparency and public participation provisions.*** Programs should publicly disclose (a) what information is captured and made available to different stakeholders; (b) local stakeholder consultation requirements (if applicable); and (c) public comments provisions and requirements, and how they are considered (if applicable). Conduct public comment periods and transparently disclose all approved quantification methodologies.

---

[1] ICAO. 2019. *CORSIA Emissions Unit Eligibility Criteria*. March. https://www.icao.int/environmental-protection/CORSIA/Documents/ICAO_Document_09.pdf.

(ix) ***Safeguards system.*** Programs should have in place safeguards to address environmental and social risks. These safeguards should be publicly disclosed.

(x) ***Sustainable development criteria.*** Programs should publicly disclose the sustainable development criteria used, for example, how this contributes to achieving a country's stated sustainable development priorities, and any provisions for monitoring, reporting, and verification.

(xi) ***Avoidance of double counting, issuance, and claiming.*** Programs should provide information on how they address double counting, issuance, and claiming in the context of evolving national and international regimes for carbon markets and emissions trading.

Carbon offset credit integrity assessment criteria. There are a number of generally agreed principles that have been broadly applied across both regulatory and voluntary offset credit programs to address environmental and social integrity. These principles hold that offset credit programs should deliver credits that represent emissions reductions, avoidance, or sequestration that

(i) are additional;

(ii) are based on a realistic and credible baseline;

(iii) are quantified, monitored, reported, and verified;

(iv) have a clear and transparent chain of custody;

(v) represent permanent emissions reductions;

(vi) assess and mitigate against potential increase in emissions elsewhere;

(vii) are only counted once toward a mitigation obligation; and

(viii) do no net harm.

Eligibility criteria should apply at the program level, as the expertise and resources needed to develop and implement ICAO emissions criteria at a methodology and project level is likely to be considerable.

(i) **Eligibility Criterion: Carbon offset programs must generate units that represent emissions reductions, avoidance, or removals that are additional.** Additionality means that that the carbon offset credits represent greenhouse gas (GHG) emissions reductions or carbon sequestration or removals that exceed any GHG reduction or removals required by law, regulation, or legally binding mandate, and that exceed any GHG reductions or removals that would otherwise occur in a conservative, business-as-usual scenario. Eligible offset credit programs should clearly demonstrate that the program has procedures in place to assess/test for additionality and that those procedures provide a reasonable assurance that the emissions reductions would not have occurred in the absence of the offset program. If programs predefine certain activities as automatically additional (e.g., through a "positive list" of eligible project types), then they have to provide clear evidence on how the activity was determined to be additional. The criteria for such positive lists should be publicly disclosed and conservative. If programs do not use positive lists, then project's additionality and baseline setting should be assessed by an accredited and independent third-party verification entity and reviewed by the program.

(ii) **Eligibility Criterion: Carbon offset credits must be based on a realistic and credible baseline.** Offset credits should be issued against a realistic, defensible, and conservative baseline estimation of emissions. The baseline is the level of emissions that would have occurred assuming a conservative business-as-usual emissions trajectory, i.e., emissions without the emissions reduction activity or offset project. Baselines and underlying assumptions must be publicly disclosed.

(iii) ***Eligibility Criterion: Carbon offset credits must be quantified, monitored, reported, and verified.*** Emissions reductions should be calculated in a manner that is conservative and transparent. Offset credits should be based on accurate measurements and quantification methods/protocols. Monitoring, measuring, and reporting of both the emissions reduction activity and the actual emissions reduction from the project should, at a minimum, be conducted at specified intervals throughout the duration of the crediting period. Emissions reductions should be measured and verified by an accredited and independent third-party verification entity. Ex-post verification of the project's emissions must be required in advance of issuance of offset credits. Programs that conduct ex-ante issuance (e.g., issuance of offset units before the emissions reductions and/or carbon sequestration have occurred and been verified by a third-party) should not be eligible. Transparent measurement and reporting is essential, and units from offsetting programs/projects eligible in a global market-based measure should only come from those that require independent, ex-post verification.

(iv) ***Eligibility Criterion: Carbon offset credits must have a clear and transparent chain of custody within the offset program.*** Offset credits should be assigned an identification number that can be tracked from when the unit is issued through to its transfer or use (cancellation or retirement) via a registry system(s).

(v) ***Eligibility Criterion: Permanence.*** Carbon offset credits must represent emissions reductions, avoidance, or carbon sequestration that are permanent. If there is risk of reductions or removals being reversed, then either (a) such credits are not eligible or (b) mitigation measures are in place to monitor, mitigate, and compensate any material incidence of non-permanence.

(vi) ***Eligibility Criterion: A system must have measures in place to assess and mitigate incidences of material leakage.*** Offset credits should be generated from projects that do not cause emissions to materially increase elsewhere (this concept is also known as leakage). Offset credit programs should have an established process for assessing and mitigating leakage of emissions that may result from the implementation of an offset project or program.

(vii) ***Eligibility Criterion: Are only counted once toward a mitigation obligation.*** Measures must be in place to avoid:

   (a) Double issuance (which occurs if more than one unit is issued for the same emissions or emissions reduction).

   (b) Double use (which occurs when the same issued unit is used twice, for example, if a unit is duplicated in registries).

   (c) Double claiming (which occurs if the same emissions reduction is counted twice by both the buyer and the seller (i.e., counted toward the climate change mitigation effort of both an airline and the host country of the emissions reduction activity)). In order to prevent double claiming, eligible programs should require and demonstrate that host countries of emissions reduction activities agree to account for any offset units issued as a result of those activities such that double claiming does not occur between the airline and the host country of the emissions reduction activity.

(iv) ***Eligibility Criterion: Carbon offset credits must represent emissions reductions, avoidance, or carbon sequestration from projects that do no net harm.*** Offset projects should not violate local, state or provincial, and national or international regulations or obligations. Offset programs should show how they comply with social and environmental safeguards and should publicly disclose which institutions, processes, and procedures are used to implement, monitor, and enforce safeguards to identify, assess, and manage environmental and social risks.

APPENDIX 2
Double-Counting Provisions

Carbon Offsetting and Reduction Scheme for International Aviation Double-Counting Provisions

The Carbon Offsetting and Reduction Scheme for International Aviation (CORSIA) has addressed double-counting risks through requirements on eligible programs. Table A1 is an extract from the Supplementary Information for Assessment of Emissions Unit Programs, which provides further guidelines on host country attestation and other provisions to avoid double claiming.[2]

Table A1: Carbon Offsetting and Reduction Scheme for International Aviation Host Country Attestation and Double-Counting Provisions

3.7.8 Host country attestation to the avoidance of double claiming	Only emissions units originating in countries that have attested to their intention to properly account for the use of the units toward offsetting obligations under the CORSIA, as specified in paragraph (and subparagraphs of) 3.7.9, should be eligible for use in the CORSIA. The program should obtain or require activity proponents to obtain and provide to the program, written attestation from the host country's national focal point or focal point's designee.[a] The attestation should specify, and describe any steps taken, to prevent mitigation associated with units used by operators under CORSIA from also being claimed toward a host country's national mitigation target(s) or pledge(s). Host country attestations should be obtained and made publicly available prior to the use of units from the host country in the CORSIA.
3.7.9. Double-claiming procedures	The program should have procedures in place requiring that activities take approach(es) described in these subparagraphs to prevent double claiming, which attestations should confirm.
3.7.9.1	Emissions units are created where mitigation is not also counted toward national target(s)/pledge(s)/mitigation contributions/mitigation commitments.
3.7.9.2.	Mitigation from emissions units used by operators under the CORSIA is appropriately accounted for by the host country when claiming achievement of its target(s)/pledges(s)/mitigation contributions/mitigation commitments, in line with the relevant and applicable international provisions.
3.7.9.3	If program procedures provide for the use of method(s) to avoid double claiming which are not listed above, the GMTF, or other appropriate technical expert body, should evaluate and make a recommendation regarding the sufficiency of the approach prior to any final determination of the program's eligibility.

CORSIA = Carbon Offsetting and Reduction Scheme for International Aviation, GMTF = Global Market-Based Measure Task Force, ICAO = International Civil Aviation Organization.

[a] Agency responsible for a host country's national emissions inventory reporting (National Focal Point), including under the Paris Agreement.

Source: ICAO. 2020. Technical Advisory Body. Programme Application Form, Appendix A. Supplementary Information for Assessment of Emissions Unit Programs.

---

[2] ICAO. 2020. Technical Advisory Body. Programme Application Form, Appendix A. Supplementary Information for Assessment of Emissions Unit Programs.

For countries that have announced Cancun pledges, supplying certified emission reductions (CERs) for CORSIA would mean that they need to attest that the emission reductions are not used for the Cancun pledge. The Cancun pledges are currently not on the agenda, so this issue becomes more important in relation to the Paris Agreement where countries have set targets through their nationally determined contributions (NDCs).

Paris Agreement Double-Counting Provisions and Implication for the Carbon Offsetting and Reduction Scheme for International Aviation

The regulatory framework for avoiding double counting under the Paris Agreement will have impacts for countries that are Parties to the Paris Agreement and participate in CORSIA. The exact content of this framework is still in play. While the main part of the Rulebook operationalizes the Paris Agreement, Parties failed to reach agreement on the Article 6 rules at the 24th Conference of the Parties (COP24) in 2018 and they also failed to reach agreement at COP25 in Madrid in 2019. Instead, the Parties agreed to continue work at the next meeting of the Subsidiary Body for Scientific and Technological Advice (SBSTA)[3] with the aim of adopting the guidance and rules at COP26.[4]

Article 6 of the Paris Agreement enables Parties to voluntarily cooperate to implement their NDCs and pursue higher ambition through the use of:

(i) internationally transferred mitigation outcomes (ITMOs) under Article 6.2;
(ii) a new mechanism under Article 6.4 that many expect to contain features that build upon the project-based mechanisms under the Kyoto Protocol—the Clean Development Mechanism (CDM) and Joint Implementation (JI); and
(iii) a framework for nonmarket approaches under Article 6.8, which is intended to capture actions that drive cost-effective mitigation (and adaptation) without relying on market-based approaches or mechanisms that use transferable or tradable exchange media.

For each of these three approaches, Parties need to reach agreement on guidance; rules, modalities, and procedures; and a work program. The key element in these negotiations that relate to CORSIA is the guidance relating to accounting under Article 6.2.

Double counting of emissions reductions credits/units from international market mechanisms leads to the risk of discrepancy between actual and reported global emissions, which may reduce the global ambition of NDCs to achieve the Paris Agreement goals. The issue of double counting has been discussed between countries and stakeholders, and a mandate to avoid double counting was reflected in the Paris Agreement.[5] Article 4.13 of the Paris Agreement states:

> Parties shall account for their nationally determined contributions. In accounting for anthropogenic emissions and removals corresponding to their nationally determined contributions, Parties shall promote environmental integrity, transparency, accuracy, completeness, comparability and

---

[3] At this point, the negotiations at the technical level (SBSTA 52) are postponed to 2021 due to coronavirus disease (COVID-19).
[4] COP26 was scheduled to be held in Glasgow in November 2020 but was postponed to 2021 due to COVID-19.
[5] A. Amellina and Y. Mizuno. 2018. Institutional Arrangements for Reporting the Use of Market Mechanisms Under the Enhanced Transparency Framework to Avoid Double Counting. *Institute for Global Environment Strategies Working Paper.* May. https://www.iges.or.jp/en/pub/institutional-arrangements-reporting-use/en.

consistency, and ensure the avoidance of double counting, in accordance with guidance adopted by the Conference of the Parties serving as the meeting of the Parties to this Agreement.

A predicament is that the requirement for general accounting does not apply for the first NDC periods. Paragraph 32 of the decision to adopt the Paris Agreement and establish the work plan for its implementation states, referring to accounting requirements in paragraph 31, that:

> 32. Decides that Parties shall apply the guidance referred to in paragraph 31 above to the second and subsequent nationally determined contributions and that Parties may elect to apply such guidance to their first nationally determined contribution....

An enhanced transparency framework under the Paris Agreement was designed to obtain necessary information from the Parties to understand where Parties are in their efforts to meet their NDCs targets, so that global efforts to meet the 2°C and 1.5°C targets can be tracked, but as previously indicated, the formal requirement to account for the emissions does not apply immediately. What is important though is that if countries use carbon market mechanisms involving the transfer of mitigation outcomes, then there must be accounting. Article 6.2 states:

> Parties shall, where engaging on a voluntary basis in cooperative approaches that involve the use of internationally transferred mitigation outcomes towards nationally determined contributions, promote sustainable development and ensure environmental integrity and transparency, including in governance, and shall apply robust accounting to ensure, inter alia, the avoidance of double counting, consistent with guidance adopted by the Conference of the Parties serving as the meeting of the Parties to this Agreement.

The decision on the adoption of the Paris Agreement introduced using "corresponding adjustments" as a means for avoiding double counting.[6]

> Requests the SBSTA to develop and recommend the guidance referred to under Art 6.2, of the PA for consideration and adoption by the CMA1, including guidance to ensure that double counting is avoided on the basis of a corresponding adjustment by Parties for both anthropogenic emissions by sources and removals by sinks covered by their NDCs under the PA....

This request is still under discussions and the question to what extent use of carbon credits for CORSIA will be subject to the guidance and accounting provisions of Article 6.2 is still open. The last draft decision text from COP25 (third iteration of Presidency text,[7] building on previous similar formulations, stipulates that corresponding adjustments also should be made when ITMOs are involved in "use for other international mitigation purposes"):

> Where a participating Party authorizes mitigation outcomes for other international mitigation purposes, it shall apply a corresponding adjustment, consistent with this guidance, for first transfer, whether or not the mitigation outcomes have been internationally transferred.

This prevents double counting of carbon credits used towards CORSIA by ensuring they will not also be counted towards a Party's NDC. This would take place regardless of program or mechanism to be used. For the first voluntary period, CORSIA use of carbon offsets will not be subject to Article 6.2 guidance. The reason is that the

---

[6] United Nations Framework Convention on Climate Change (UNFCCC). 2016. Decision 1.CP/21, paragraph 36. https://unfccc.int/resource/docs/2015/cop21/eng/10a01.pdf#page=2.

[7] UNFCCC. 2019. Proposal by the President: Draft CMA Decision on Guidance on Cooperative Approaches Referred to in Article 6, Paragraph 2, of the Paris Agreement. Madrid. Section D, para. 16. https://unfccc.int/sites/default/files/resource/DT.CMA2_.i11a.v3_0.pdf.

offsets already have been issued, thus not representing the first transfer of an ITMO. The eligible vintages stem from the period before the Article 6.2 guidance will apply.

The similar rules are proposed for the new mechanism under Article 6.4 that will replace the CDM[8]

> A host Party shall apply an adjustment for A6.4ERs consistent with chapter IX. above (Avoiding the double use of emission reductions) and decision X/CMA.2 (guidance on cooperative approaches referred to in Article 6, paragraph 2, of the Paris Agreement).

The proposed provisions for Article 6.4 also require the host country to authorize the use of A6.4ERs for international purposes:

> The host Party shall provide to the Supervisory Body the authorization for A6.4ERs issued for the activity to be internationally transferred for use towards NDCs or to be used for other international mitigation purposes or for other purposes, if the Party decides to do so, and a statement as to whether a corresponding adjustment will be applied by the host Party for A6.4ERs in accordance with chapter 10 below (Avoiding the use of emission reductions by more than one Party.... [9]

The Article 6 provisions address the risk of double claiming (which is not addressed in CDM or voluntary standards) and also contribute to the possibility of avoiding double issuance and double use since the information on authorization of ITMO transfer and corresponding adjustments will be publicly available. As mitigation outcomes become a national asset that possibly are needed for NDC achievement, the supply of offsets in the post-2020 period could become limited compared to the supply available for the first pilot phase of CORSIA. However, this will largely depend on whether or not access to pre-2020 vintages will be granted for the coming CORSIA periods.

---

[8] UNFCCC. 2019. Proposal by the President: Draft CMA Decision on the Rules, Modalities and Procedures for the Mechanism Established by Article 6, Paragraph 4, of the Paris Agreement. Madrid. Section X, para. 71. https://unfccc.int/sites/default/files/resource/CMA2_11b_DT_Art.6.4_.pdf.

[9] UNFCCC. 2019. Draft Text on Matters relating to Article 6 of the Paris Agreement: Rules, modalities and procedures for the mechanism established by Article 6, paragraph 4, of the Paris Agreement Version 3 of 15 December 1:10 hrs. https://unfccc.int/documents/204686.

References

Amellina, A. and Y. Mizuno. 2018. Institutional Arrangements for Reporting the Use of Market Mechanisms Under the Enhanced Transparency Framework to Avoid Double Counting. *Institute for Global Environment Strategies Working Paper*. May. https://www.iges.or.jp/en/pub/institutional-arrangements-reporting-use/en.

Anjaparidze, G. 2019. The Extraordinary Climate Agreement on International Aviation: An Airline Industry Perspective. *Policy Brief: Harvard Project on Climate Agreements*. October 2019. https://www.belfercenter.org/publication/extraordinary-climate-agreement-international-aviation-airline-industry-perspective.

———. 2019. Change of CORSIA. Airline Routes & Ground Services Magazine. Winter 2019. p. 44. https://airlinergs.com/issue/winter-2019/.

———. 2019. Why is UNFCCC COP25 Important for International Aviation? *International Institute for Sustainable Development*. 3 December. https://sdg.iisd.org/commentary/guest-articles/why-is-unfccc-cop-25-important-for-international-aviation/.

Air Transport Action Group. 2020. Aviation Benefits Beyond Borders. Sustainable Aviation Fuel. https://aviationbenefits.org/environmental-efficiency/climate-action/sustainable-aviation-fuel.

Delta Air Lines. 2020. Delta Commits $1 Billion to Become First Carbon Neutral Airline Globally. 14 February. https://news.delta.com/delta-commits-1-billion-become-first-carbon-neutral-airline-globally.

Dichter, A. et al. 2020. How Airlines Can Chart a Path to Zero-Carbon Flying. *McKinsey & Company*. 13 May. https://www.mckinsey.com/industries/travel-logistics-and-transport-infrastructure/our-insights/how-airlines-can-chart-a-path-to-zero-carbon-flying.

European Investment Bank (EIB). 2020. 2nd EIB Climate Survey: Citizens' Commitment to Fight Climate Change in 2020. https://www.eib.org/en/surveys/2nd-citizen-survey/new-years-resolutions.htm.

European Commission. 2020. Emission Trading: Greenhouse Gas Emissions Reduced by 8.7% in 2019. 4 May. https://ec.europa.eu/clima/news/emissions-trading-greenhouse-gas-emissions-reduced-87-2019_en.

Food and Agriculture Organization of the United Nations. 2016. *The Agriculture Sectors in the Intended Nationally Determined Contributions: Analysis,* by R. Strohmaier et al. Environment and Natural Resources Management Working Paper No. 62. Rome. http://www.fao.org/3/a-i5687e.pdf.

GreenAir. 2020. IATA calls for change in CORSIA baseline to protect airlines from future higher offsetting requirements. 3 April. https://www.greenaironline.com/news.php?viewStory=2685.

International Civil Aviation Organization (ICAO). 2020. *Document: CORSIA States for Chapter 3 State Pairs*. July. https://www.icao.int/environmental-protection/CORSIA/Pages/state-pairs.aspx.

———. 2020. ICAO Council agrees to safeguard adjustment for CORSIA in light of COVID-19 pandemic. 30 June. https://www.icao.int/Newsroom/Pages/ICAO-Council-agrees-to-the-safeguard-adjustment-for-CORSIA-in-light-of-COVID19-pandemic.aspx.

———. 2020. *Effects of Novel Coronavirus on Civil Aviation: Economic Impact Analysis*. 25 May. https://www.icao.int/sustainability/Documents/COVID-19/ICAO%20COVID%202020%2005%2025%20Economic%20Impact.pdf.

———. 2020. Technical Advisory Body. Programme Application Form, Appendix A. Supplementary Information for Assessment of Emissions Unit Programs.

———. 2019. Destination Green: The Next Chapter. *ICAO Environmental Report 2019: Aviation and Environment*. Chapter 1. https://www.icao.int/environmental-protection/Pages/envrep2019.aspx.

———. 2019 - 2007. Annual Reports of the Council. Air Transport Statistical Results. https://www.icao.int/about-icao/Pages/annual-reports.aspx

———. 2019. Resolution A40-18: Consolidated Statement of Continuing ICAO Policies and Practices Related to Environmental Protection - Climate Change. Assembly 40th Session. Montreal. 24 September to 4 October. https://www.icao.int/Meetings/a40/Documents/Resolutions/a40_res_prov_en.pdf.

———. 2019. *CORSIA Emissions Unit Eligibility Criteria*. March. https://www.icao.int/environmental-protection/CORSIA/Documents/ICAO_Document_09.pdf.

———. 2019. CORSIA Frequently Asked Questions. 31 October. https://www.icao.int/environmental-protection/CORSIA/Documents/CORSIA_FAQs_October%202019_final.pdf.

———. 2018. Annex 16: Environmental Protection, Volume IV: Carbon Offsetting and Reduction Scheme for International Aviation. 27 June. https://www.icao.int/environmental-protection/CORSIA/Pages/SARPs-Annex-16-Volume-IV.aspx.

———. 2018. Doc 9501: Environmental Technical Manual. Volume III—Procedures for the CO_2 Emissions Certification of Aeroplanes. Montreal. https://www.icao.int/environmental-protection/Documents/Doc_9501_ETM_Vol_III_SGAR%202017.pdf.

International Airline Group (IAG). 2019. IAG Backs Net Zero Emissions by 2050. *Press Release*. 10 October. https://www.iairgroup.com/en/newsroom/press-releases/newsroom-listing/2019/net-zero-emissions.

International Air Transport Association (IATA). 2020. COVID-19 Updated Impact Assessment. 14 April. https://www.iata.org/en/iata-repository/publications/economic-reports/covid-fourth-impact-assessment/.

IATA. 2020. COVID-19 Outlook for Air Travel in the Next 5 Years. 13 May. https://www.iata.org/en/iata-repository/publications/economic-reports/covid-19-outlook-for-air-travel-in-the-next-5-years/.

———. Aircraft Technology Roadmap to 2050. Geneva. https://www.iata.org/contentassets/8d19e716636a47c184e7221c77563c93/technology20roadmap20to20205020no20foreword.pdf.

References

———. 2019. Airline Industry Economic Performance. June. https://www.iata.org/en/iata-repository/publications/economic-reports/airline-industry-economic-performance---december-2019---data-tables/

Organisation for Economic Co-operation and Development (OECD). 2020. Estimated Air Transport CO_2 Emissions. https://stats.oecd.org/Index.aspx?DataSetCode=AIRTRANS_CO2.

———. 2020. Prevailing Country Risk Classification. https://www.oecd.org/trade/topics/export-credits/arrangement-and-sector-understandings/financing-terms-and-conditions/country-risk-classification/.

Qing, T. 2018. Introduction on China Certified Emission Reductions. Presentation during the ICAO Seminar on Carbon Markets. Montreal, Canada. 7 Feb. https://www.icao.int/Meetings/carbonmarkets/Documents/01_Session2_Qing_CCER.pdf.

United Nations Environment Programme (UNEP). 2019. Emissions Gap Report 2019. Nairobi.

United Nations Framework Convention on Climate Change (UNFCCC). 2019. Proposal by the President: Draft CMA Decision on Guidance on Cooperative Approaches Referred to in Article 6, Paragraph 2, of the Paris Agreement. Madrid. Section D, para. 16. https://unfccc.int/sites/default/files/resource/DT.CMA2_.i11a.v3_0.pdf.

UNFCCC. 2019. Proposal by the President: Draft CMA Decision on the Rules, Modalities and Procedures for the Mechanism Established by Article 6, Paragraph 4, of the Paris Agreement. Madrid. Section X, para. 71. https://unfccc.int/sites/default/files/resource/CMA2_11b_DT_Art.6.4_.pdf.

———. 2016. Updated Synthesis Report on the Aggregate Effect of INDCs. 2 May. https://unfccc.int/resource/docs/2016/cop22/eng/02.pdf.

———. 2015. Submission of the Republic of Korea, Intended Nationally Determined Contribution. 30 June.

———. 2015. Paris Agreement to the United Nations Framework Convention on Climate Change. Paris. 30 November–13 December. https://unfccc.int/sites/default/files/english_paris_agreement.pdf.

———. 1997. Kyoto Protocol to the United Nations Framework Convention on Climate Change. Kyoto. 1–10 December. https://unfccc.int/sites/default/files/resource/docs/cop3/l07a01.pdf.

World Bank. 2007. *Uzbekistan Carbon Finance for New Project: A Primer*. J. Ebinger and G. Anjaparidze. 14 January. http://documents.worldbank.org/curated/en/917621468338451727/pdf/707460ESW0P10000brief0final0011807.pdf.

www.ingramcontent.com/pod-product-compliance
Lightning Source LLC
Chambersburg PA
CBHW060941170426
43195CB00026B/2999